Sustainable Practices in Warehousing

Table of Contents

Part I: Understanding Sustainability in Warehousing   5

Introduction to Sustainability in Warehousing   6

The Triple Bottom Line in Warehousing   13

Regulations and Standards for Sustainable Warehousing   22

Challenges and Opportunities in Sustainable Warehousing   30

Part II: Green Building Design and Construction   38

Sustainable Warehouse Design Principles   39

Energy-Efficient Construction Materials   48

Renewable Energy Solutions in Warehousing   58

Energy Management in Warehouse Operations   66

Part III: Optimizing Warehouse Operations   75

Water Conservation in Warehouses   76

Waste Management in Warehousing   84

Efficient Material Handling and Storage   93

Part IV: Technology for Sustainable Warehousing   102

Role of Automation and IoT in Sustainability	103
Big Data and Analytics for Green Warehousing	111
Smart Warehouse Management Systems (WMS)	119
Eco-Friendly Transportation Strategies	128
Part V: Sustainable Transportation and Logistics	136
Carbon Footprint Reduction in Warehousing	137
Part VI: Workforce and Community Engagement	146
Building a Culture of Sustainability	147
Community and Stakeholder Engagement	156
Part VII: Circular Economy and Warehousing	165
Adopting Circular Economy Principles	166
Repair, Refurbish, and Resell Initiatives	175
Part VIII: Future of Sustainable Warehousing	183
Emerging Trends in Sustainable Warehousing	184
Resilience and Adaptability in Warehousing	192
Integrating ESG Goals in Warehousing	201
Measuring and Reporting Sustainability Performance	211
Conclusion: The Path Forward	221

Part I: Understanding Sustainability in Warehousing

Introduction to Sustainability in Warehousing

Warehousing, the silent backbone of global commerce, is more than just a place where goods are stored. It is an intricate hub of activity where supply meets demand, logistics meets efficiency, and increasingly, where sustainability meets responsibility. As businesses grapple with the pressing realities of climate change, resource depletion, and societal expectations, the role of sustainability in warehousing has emerged as a cornerstone for future operations. This chapter delves into the essence of sustainability in warehousing, the evolving global trends in the industry, and the profound environmental, social, and economic impacts it carries.

1. Definition and Importance of Sustainability

In the simplest terms, sustainability refers to practices that meet the needs of today without compromising the ability of future generations to meet theirs. In the context of warehousing, it involves a holistic approach that balances environmental stewardship, social responsibility, and economic efficiency. It is not merely about reducing waste or cutting energy costs; it is about redefining operations to ensure long-term viability in harmony with the planet and society.

1.1 Defining Sustainability in Warehousing

Imagine a warehouse bustling with activity—robots sorting packages, forklifts gliding through aisles, and climate-controlled zones ensuring perishable goods remain

\fresh. Now envision this warehouse powered by solar panels, its walls insulated with recycled materials, and its operations guided by smart systems that optimize energy use. This is the essence of a sustainable warehouse.

Sustainability in warehousing manifests in several ways:

Energy Efficiency: Minimizing energy consumption through advanced lighting systems, efficient HVAC setups, and renewable energy sources.

Resource Optimization: Utilizing resources such as water, packaging materials, and space in a way that minimizes waste and maximizes utility.

Waste Reduction: Adopting practices like recycling, composting, and efficient inventory management to minimize landfill contributions.

Social Responsibility: Ensuring safe working conditions, fair wages, and positive community impact.

1.2 Importance of Sustainability in Warehousing

Why does sustainability in warehousing matter? The answer lies in the intricate web of benefits it offers—environmental preservation, cost savings, compliance, reputation enhancement, and risk reduction.

Environmental Preservation:

Warehousing, with its energy-intensive operations and significant waste output, contributes to environmental degradation. Adopting sustainable practices such as renewable energy, efficient lighting, and waste recycling helps mitigate these impacts, ensuring a healthier planet for future generations.

Cost Efficiency:

Contrary to the misconception that sustainability is expensive, it often leads to cost savings. For instance, energy-efficient lighting like LED bulbs and renewable energy systems may have higher upfront costs but drastically reduce long-term energy expenses.

Regulatory Compliance:

Governments worldwide are implementing stringent environmental regulations. Sustainable warehousing ensures compliance with these laws, protecting businesses from fines and reputational damage.

Customer Expectations:

In today's marketplace, consumers are increasingly drawn to brands that prioritize sustainability. Warehousing practices that align with green values enhance brand reputation and customer loyalty.

Risk Mitigation:

Sustainability builds resilience. By reducing dependence on finite resources and aligning with societal expectations, sustainable warehouses are better equipped to handle future disruptions, whether environmental, regulatory, or social.

2. Overview of Global Warehousing Trends

Warehousing has evolved from being simple storage facilities to dynamic hubs of technology, logistics, and innovation. With this evolution has come an increased focus on sustainability as businesses strive to balance operational efficiency with environmental and social responsibilities.

2.1 Growth of Warehousing

The warehousing industry is witnessing explosive growth, fueled by the rise of e-commerce, globalization, and consumer demand for faster delivery. Giant distribution centers now dot the globe, from Amazon's sprawling fulfillment hubs to urban micro-warehouses catering to last-mile delivery.

However, this growth comes at a cost. Energy consumption, greenhouse gas emissions, and resource use have surged alongside warehouse expansion, highlighting the urgent need for sustainable solutions.

2.2 Energy and Resource Demands

Modern warehouses are no longer just storage spaces; they are high-tech centers equipped with automated sorting systems, climate-controlled zones, and round-the-clock lighting. This evolution, while enhancing efficiency, has drastically increased energy demands. Cold storage facilities, in particular, are significant energy guzzlers, consuming up to 10 times more energy than standard warehouses.

Similarly, resource demands in warehousing extend beyond energy. Water usage, packaging materials, and land development are critical considerations, with significant environmental implications if not managed sustainably.

2.3 Regional Trends

The global nature of warehousing brings diverse trends and challenges:

North America and Europe: Sustainability is a priority, with green certifications such as LEED (Leadership in Energy and Environmental Design) driving construction and operational practices.

Asia-Pacific: The region's rapid industrial growth has led to an increase in warehousing facilities, presenting opportunities for sustainability initiatives to take root.

Developing Economies: In regions with fewer regulations, warehousing growth often comes at the expense of environmental and social considerations. However, rising awareness and international partnerships are beginning to drive change.

3. Environmental, Social, and Economic Impacts of Warehousing

Warehousing operations, while vital to global trade, leave a profound imprint on the environment, society, and economy. Understanding these impacts is essential for crafting sustainable solutions.

3.1 Environmental Impacts

Energy Use and Emissions:

Warehouses are energy-intensive, relying on lighting, HVAC systems, and automation. This reliance often translates to high carbon emissions, especially in facilities dependent on fossil fuels.

Waste Generation:

The sheer volume of packaging materials, damaged goods, and outdated equipment generated by warehouses poses a significant waste management challenge. Unsustainable practices exacerbate this issue, leading to increased landfill use.

Land Use:

Large warehouses require extensive land, often encroaching on natural habitats. Urban warehouses, while convenient, can strain local infrastructure and ecosystems.

3.2 Social Impacts

Worker Well-Being:

Warehousing jobs are often physically demanding, with risks of injuries from repetitive tasks or heavy machinery. Ensuring ergonomic designs and safety protocols is crucial for worker health.

Community Engagement:

Warehouses impact local communities through traffic, noise, and pollution. Sustainable warehouses address these concerns, fostering positive relationships with surrounding areas.

Social Equity:

Fair wages, equal opportunities, and safe working conditions are pillars of socially responsible warehousing.

3.3 Economic Impacts

Cost Implications:

Inefficient warehouses face high operational costs, from excessive energy bills to waste disposal fees. Sustainable practices reduce these expenses, enhancing profitability.

Market Competitiveness:

Sustainability is a differentiator in the marketplace. Businesses that adopt green warehousing practices often attract environmentally conscious partners and consumers.

Supply Chain Efficiency:

Sustainable warehousing enhances overall supply chain performance by reducing waste, optimizing resources, and minimizing disruptions.

Sustainability in warehousing is not just a trend; it is a necessity. As global commerce continues to grow, so too does the need for responsible practices that balance efficiency with environmental and social considerations. From energy use and waste generation to worker safety and community relations, every aspect of warehousing has a role to play in creating a sustainable future. By embracing sustainability, warehouses can transform from contributors to environmental degradation into pioneers of a greener, more equitable world.

The Triple Bottom Line in Warehousing

Warehousing, as a pivotal component of supply chain operations, is more than a logistical necessity; it is a dynamic hub where goods, people, and processes converge. Modern warehousing not only influences economic outcomes but also plays a significant role in environmental stewardship and social responsibility. The concept of the Triple Bottom Line (TBL)—people, planet, and profit—provides a framework for assessing and balancing these three critical dimensions within warehousing operations. This chapter explores the essence of the TBL in warehousing, emphasizing the challenges and strategies for achieving harmony among people, the planet, and profit.

4. Balancing People, Planet, and Profit

4.1 The Essence of the Triple Bottom Line

The Triple Bottom Line moves beyond traditional profit-centered business models to incorporate social and environmental dimensions into decision-making processes. The philosophy acknowledges that businesses do not exist in isolation; they operate within ecosystems where human welfare, environmental health, and economic success are deeply interconnected.

In the warehousing context:

People refers to the human aspects, including employee well-being, community engagement, and fair labor practices.

Planet encompasses environmental considerations such as energy efficiency, waste management, and carbon footprint reduction.

Profit signifies financial performance but extends to long-term economic sustainability through resource optimization and operational efficiency.

4.2 People: The Social Dimension

Warehousing involves diverse human interactions, from employees operating machinery to communities affected by warehouse operations. Addressing the "people" aspect of TBL ensures that human welfare is prioritized alongside business efficiency.

Employee Well-Being

Warehousing jobs are often physically demanding, involving repetitive tasks, long hours, and potential hazards from heavy machinery. Ensuring worker well-being requires:

Safety Protocols: Implementing robust safety standards, providing personal protective equipment (PPE), and conducting regular safety drills.

Ergonomic Workspaces: Designing workstations and tools to minimize physical strain and enhance productivity.

Training and Development: Offering continuous skill development programs to empower employees and improve job satisfaction.

Community Engagement

Warehouses impact surrounding communities through traffic congestion, noise, and environmental changes. Sustainable warehouses foster positive relationships with local communities by:

Hosting stakeholder meetings to address community concerns.

Supporting local employment and using local suppliers.

Minimizing operational disruptions, such as noise pollution and excessive traffic.

Social Equity

Warehousing organizations must ensure equitable opportunities for all employees, regardless of gender, ethnicity, or socioeconomic background. Diverse and inclusive workplaces not only reflect social responsibility but also boost innovation and team cohesion.

4.3 Planet: The Environmental Dimension

The environmental impact of warehousing operations is significant, with challenges such as energy consumption, waste generation, and land use. Embracing the "planet" aspect of TBL requires warehouses to operate responsibly within ecological limits.

Energy Efficiency

Warehousing facilities are energy-intensive, often requiring round-the-clock lighting, climate control, and automated systems. Strategies for energy efficiency include:

Renewable Energy Integration: Installing solar panels or wind turbines to power operations.

Energy-Efficient Equipment: Replacing traditional HVAC systems and lighting with energy-saving alternatives like LED lighting and energy-efficient chillers.

Smart Systems: Utilizing energy management systems to monitor and optimize energy usage.

Waste Reduction

From packaging materials to discarded inventory, warehouses generate considerable waste. Sustainable practices involve:

Implementing recycling programs for packaging materials and outdated equipment.

Adopting reusable packaging solutions.

Reducing waste through advanced inventory management systems that minimize obsolescence and overstocking.

Biodiversity and Land Use

Large warehouses often encroach on natural habitats, altering local ecosystems. Sustainable warehouses minimize their ecological footprint by:

Building on previously developed land or brownfield sites.

Incorporating green infrastructure such as green roofs and rainwater harvesting systems.

Restoring adjacent natural habitats through tree planting and conservation efforts.

4.4 Profit: The Economic Dimension

The profitability of warehousing is essential for business continuity and growth. However, sustainability and profitability are not mutually exclusive; rather, they complement each other in a well-designed Triple Bottom Line strategy.

Operational Efficiency

Sustainable warehouses achieve profitability through efficiency:

Reducing energy and water costs through efficient systems.

Streamlining workflows to minimize labor costs and improve productivity.

Adopting advanced technologies like robotics and warehouse management systems (WMS) to enhance accuracy and reduce errors.

Market Competitiveness

Consumers and business partners increasingly prefer organizations that demonstrate sustainability. Warehouses that prioritize TBL often gain competitive advantages such as:

Enhanced brand reputation.

Attracting environmentally conscious customers and partners.

Meeting stringent compliance requirements, avoiding fines, and securing long-term contracts.

Long-Term Resilience

Sustainable practices mitigate risks, from regulatory penalties to resource scarcity, ensuring long-term economic viability.

For instance, adopting renewable energy reduces vulnerability to fossil fuel price volatility.

5. The Role of Warehousing in Sustainable Supply Chains

Warehousing is a critical link in supply chains, influencing how goods are stored, managed, and distributed. The sustainability of supply chains heavily depends on the practices adopted by warehousing operations.

5.1 Warehousing as a Strategic Node

As a central node in supply chains, warehouses play a strategic role in aligning operations with sustainability goals:

Inventory Management: Efficient inventory systems prevent overstocking and obsolescence, reducing waste and associated environmental impacts.

Consolidation Centers: Warehouses act as consolidation hubs, optimizing transportation and reducing carbon emissions.

5.2 Collaborative Opportunities

Sustainable supply chains thrive on collaboration. Warehouses can drive sustainability by:

Partnering with Green Suppliers: Ensuring that upstream and downstream supply chain partners adhere to sustainability standards.

Implementing Reverse Logistics: Facilitating the return, repair, and recycling of products to minimize waste.

Sharing Resources: Adopting shared warehouse facilities to optimize space usage and reduce environmental impacts.

5.3 Leveraging Technology for Sustainability

Technology is an enabler of sustainability in warehousing and supply chains:

IoT Sensors: Monitoring energy consumption, equipment performance, and environmental conditions in real-time.

Blockchain Technology: Ensuring transparency and accountability across supply chain operations.

AI and Data Analytics: Optimizing inventory levels, demand forecasting, and route planning for efficient operations.

5.4 Case Studies in Sustainable Warehousing

Amazon's Green Initiatives:

Amazon has integrated renewable energy sources into its warehouses, committed to net-zero carbon by 2040, and employs sustainable packaging solutions to reduce waste.

IKEA's Circular Approach:

IKEA's warehouses focus on reverse logistics and product recycling, aligning with the company's broader goal of becoming fully circular by 2030.

Prologis Green Buildings:

Prologis, a leading warehouse developer, emphasizes green building designs certified by LEED standards, integrating energy-efficient systems and eco-friendly materials.

The Triple Bottom Line framework underscores the necessity of balancing social, environmental, and economic priorities in warehousing. As an integral part of sustainable supply chains, warehouses hold immense potential to drive meaningful change by adopting practices that respect people, protect the planet, and ensure profitability. By embracing the TBL approach, warehouses can transition from being cost centers to strategic assets that contribute to a sustainable and resilient global economy. Through technology, innovation, and collaboration, the warehousing industry can lead the way in shaping a greener, fairer, and more prosperous future.

Regulations and Standards for Sustainable Warehousing

As the demand for sustainable practices grows, regulations and standards are evolving to ensure environmental protection, social responsibility, and economic balance in warehousing operations. Complying with these frameworks not only ensures legal adherence but also enhances operational efficiency and reputation. This chapter provides a comprehensive exploration of key global and regional sustainability regulations and certifications relevant to green warehousing.

Key Global and Regional Sustainability Regulations

1. The Importance of Regulatory Compliance

Warehousing operations impact air quality, water resources, energy consumption, and waste management. Regulatory compliance ensures that these impacts are minimized and that warehouses contribute positively to sustainable development goals (SDGs). Non-compliance can result in fines, legal action, and reputational damage, making adherence crucial for long-term success.

2. Global Sustainability Regulations

2.1 The Paris Agreement

Adopted in 2015, the Paris Agreement aims to limit global warming to below 2°C. Warehousing operations must contribute by reducing greenhouse gas (GHG) emissions through energy-efficient systems, renewable energy adoption, and sustainable logistics practices.

2.2 The United Nations Sustainable Development Goals (SDGs)

The SDGs provide a framework for addressing global sustainability challenges. Warehouses contribute directly to goals such as:

SDG 7: Affordable and clean energy through renewable energy adoption.

SDG 12: Responsible consumption and production by minimizing waste.

SDG 13: Climate action through carbon footprint reduction.

2.3 Basel Convention

This international treaty regulates the transboundary movement of hazardous waste. Warehouses handling such materials must comply with stringent guidelines for storage, handling, and disposal to prevent environmental contamination.

3. Regional Sustainability Regulations

3.1 European Union (EU)

EU Green Deal: Aims for carbon neutrality by 2050, with warehousing operations required to adopt energy-efficient practices and circular economy principles.

Energy Performance of Buildings Directive (EPBD): Sets standards for energy-efficient building design and operation, directly impacting warehouse construction and retrofitting.

Waste Framework Directive: Encourages recycling and waste minimization in warehousing operations.

3.2 United States

Clean Air Act (CAA): Warehouses must monitor and reduce air pollutants from machinery and HVAC systems.

Resource Conservation and Recovery Act (RCRA): Focuses on proper waste disposal and hazardous waste management.

Energy Star Program: Encourages energy-efficient practices and provides benchmarks for warehouse energy use.

3.3 Asia-Pacific Region

India's Environmental Protection Act: Regulates emissions and waste from industrial facilities, including warehouses.

China's Green Building Standards: Promotes energy-efficient and low-carbon building designs.

Japan's Energy Conservation Act: Encourages efficient use of energy in industrial facilities, including warehouses.

3.4 Other Regions

Australia's Green Star Ratings: Focuses on sustainability in building design, including warehouses.

Canada's Environmental Protection Act: Governs waste management and pollution prevention in warehousing operations.

Certifications for Green Warehousing

Achieving sustainability in warehousing often involves obtaining recognized certifications that validate green practices. These certifications not only demonstrate compliance but also offer competitive advantages, such as enhanced reputation and customer trust.

1. LEED (Leadership in Energy and Environmental Design)

LEED, developed by the U.S. Green Building Council (USGBC), is one of the most widely recognized green building certifications globally.

Key Features of LEED for Warehousing

Energy Efficiency: Encourages renewable energy use and efficient HVAC systems.

Water Conservation: Promotes rainwater harvesting and water-efficient plumbing.

Waste Management: Emphasizes recycling programs and construction waste minimization.

Indoor Environmental Quality: Ensures healthy air quality for workers through ventilation and non-toxic materials.

Benefits of LEED Certification

Lower operational costs through energy and water savings.

Enhanced employee well-being and productivity.

Higher property value and marketability.

2. ISO 14001

ISO 14001, developed by the International Organization for Standardization, focuses on environmental management systems (EMS).

Key Elements of ISO 14001

Environmental Policy: Establishing and maintaining policies aligned with sustainability goals.

Lifecycle Perspective: Assessing environmental impact throughout the lifecycle of warehousing operations.

Continuous Improvement: Regularly evaluating and improving environmental performance.

Benefits of ISO 14001 Certification

Demonstrates commitment to environmental responsibility.

Helps warehouses meet regulatory requirements efficiently.

Enhances operational efficiency through waste and resource management.

3. BREEAM (Building Research Establishment Environmental Assessment Method)

BREEAM is a European-based certification system that assesses the sustainability of building designs and operations.

Relevance to Warehousing

Encourages energy-efficient construction and operational practices.

Assesses building materials for sustainability and recyclability.

Focuses on reducing water usage and enhancing biodiversity in surrounding areas.

4. EDGE (Excellence in Design for Greater Efficiencies)

EDGE, developed by the International Finance Corporation (IFC), focuses on resource-efficient building design.

Applications in Warehousing

Promotes the use of energy-efficient equipment and renewable energy sources.

Encourages sustainable construction practices to minimize environmental impact.

Recognized in emerging markets as a cost-effective certification.

5. WELL Certification

WELL Certification focuses on the well-being of building occupants, making it relevant for warehouses with large workforces.

Key Features

Ensures high indoor air quality and ventilation.

Emphasizes ergonomic design and worker comfort.

Promotes access to natural light and thermal comfort.

6. Other Notable Certifications

Carbon Trust Standard: Recognizes efforts to reduce carbon footprints.

Green Globes: A flexible, performance-based certification for sustainable building operations.

Energy Star Certification: Evaluates energy performance and efficiency.

Regulations and certifications are indispensable tools for promoting sustainable warehousing. By adhering to global and regional regulations, warehouses contribute to broader environmental and social goals while avoiding legal and reputational risks. Similarly, achieving certifications like LEED, ISO 14001, and BREEAM validates sustainability efforts and sets organizations apart in a competitive market. Together, these frameworks help warehouses balance their impact on people, the planet, and profit, paving the way for a greener, more sustainable future.

Challenges and Opportunities in Sustainable Warehousing

The transition to sustainable warehousing presents a dual narrative of challenges and opportunities. On one hand, warehouses face barriers such as cost constraints, lack of expertise, and infrastructure limitations. On the other hand, emerging innovations, technological advancements, and shifting market expectations open up avenues for growth and improvement. This chapter delves into the key barriers to implementing sustainable practices and explores the opportunities that arise from embracing sustainability in warehousing.

Barriers to Implementing Sustainable Practices

1. High Initial Costs

One of the most significant barriers to sustainable warehousing is the high upfront investment required for eco-friendly infrastructure, energy-efficient equipment, and renewable energy installations.

Energy-Efficient Systems: Retrofitting warehouses with LED lighting, HVAC upgrades, or solar panels demands substantial capital.

Green Construction Materials: Sustainable building materials, though beneficial in the long run, often come at a premium price.

Automation and Smart Technologies: Implementing automation for energy optimization requires costly advanced technologies.

Impacts

The financial burden can deter small to medium-sized enterprises (SMEs) from adopting green practices despite long-term benefits.

2. Lack of Expertise and Awareness

Sustainability in warehousing is a relatively new concept for many businesses, leading to gaps in knowledge and expertise.

Training Needs: Workforce and management require training to adopt and manage sustainable practices effectively.

Limited Awareness: Some businesses remain unaware of potential cost savings and operational benefits derived from sustainability.

Resistance to Change: Traditional mindsets often resist shifting toward sustainable methods due to fear of disrupting established processes.

3. Infrastructure Limitations

Existing warehouses may lack the physical structure needed to support sustainable initiatives.

Retrofit Challenges: Older facilities are often not designed for energy efficiency or renewable energy installations.

Space Constraints: Limited space for green initiatives like rainwater harvesting or on-site renewable energy generation can hinder implementation.

4. Supply Chain and Vendor Issues

Sustainability in warehousing is interconnected with the broader supply chain, which can present barriers.

Supplier Alignment: Not all suppliers adhere to sustainable practices, creating gaps in the green supply chain.

Transportation Emissions: Warehouses reliant on traditional logistics methods face challenges in reducing transportation-related emissions.

5. Regulatory and Certification Complexity

Navigating the landscape of sustainability regulations and certifications can be overwhelming.

Diverse Standards: Warehouses operating in multiple regions must comply with varying regulations and standards, adding complexity.

Certification Costs: Achieving certifications such as LEED or ISO 14001 involves significant financial and administrative resources.

6. Technological and Data Barriers

While technology plays a pivotal role in sustainable warehousing, adopting and integrating it comes with challenges.

Data Integration: Collecting and analyzing data on energy use, emissions, and resource consumption requires advanced systems.

Maintenance Costs: Sustainable technologies often involve ongoing maintenance, further adding to operational costs.

Emerging Opportunities and Innovations

Despite these challenges, sustainable warehousing offers abundant opportunities to innovate, improve efficiency, and meet growing market demands.

1. Cost Savings through Efficiency

Adopting sustainable practices can lead to significant cost savings in the long term.

Energy Savings: Implementing LED lighting, motion sensors, and renewable energy systems reduces utility bills.

Reduced Waste: Practices like recycling and material optimization lower waste disposal costs.

Optimized Operations: Automation and IoT-enabled monitoring systems streamline warehouse operations, reducing resource wastage.

2. Enhanced Market Competitiveness

Sustainability is increasingly becoming a differentiating factor in competitive markets.

Consumer Demand: Growing consumer preference for environmentally responsible businesses drives the adoption of green practices.

Corporate Partnerships: Businesses prioritizing sustainability are more likely to collaborate with green-certified warehouses.

Brand Reputation: Warehouses that demonstrate environmental responsibility enhance their brand image and attract eco-conscious clients.

3. Technological Advancements

Technology is transforming sustainable warehousing, making it more accessible and efficient.

IoT and Smart Sensors: These technologies monitor energy use, optimize HVAC systems, and track emissions in real-time.

Automation: Robotic systems improve resource allocation, reduce energy consumption, and minimize human error.

Renewable Energy Integration: Solar panels, wind turbines, and geothermal systems reduce dependency on traditional energy sources.

4. Innovations in Green Building Design

Architectural and engineering advancements enable the development of highly efficient green warehouses.

Net-Zero Warehouses: Facilities designed to produce as much energy as they consume are gaining traction.

Passive Design Techniques: Natural ventilation, daylighting, and insulation reduce energy consumption in warehouses.

Sustainable Materials: The use of recycled steel, bamboo, and other green materials lowers the environmental footprint of warehouse construction.

5. Government Incentives and Support

Governments worldwide are offering incentives to encourage sustainability in warehousing.

Tax Credits: Businesses implementing energy-efficient practices often qualify for tax benefits.

Subsidies: Grants and subsidies support renewable energy installations and green retrofits.

Carbon Credits: Warehouses reducing emissions can participate in carbon trading programs to generate additional revenue.

6. Circular Economy Integration

Warehouses play a critical role in enabling circular economy practices.

Reverse Logistics: Managing the return and recycling of goods aligns with circular economy principles.

Sustainable Packaging: Warehouses adopting eco-friendly packaging contribute to waste reduction.

Resource Recovery: Warehousing operations focusing on material recovery minimize landfill contributions.

7. Collaboration and Partnerships

Collaborative efforts drive innovation and shared responsibility in sustainable warehousing.

Industry Alliances: Joining sustainability-focused industry groups accelerates knowledge sharing and innovation.

Supplier Engagement: Working closely with suppliers to adopt green practices ensures consistency across the supply chain.

Community Initiatives: Warehouses engaging with local communities to promote environmental awareness enhance social responsibility.

8. Preparing for the Future

Sustainable warehousing positions businesses to adapt to future challenges and trends.

Resilience to Regulations: Warehouses already adhering to sustainability standards are better equipped to comply with future regulations.

Adapting to Climate Change: Sustainable practices mitigate risks associated with climate change, such as resource scarcity or extreme weather.

Emerging Technologies: Warehouses investing in innovation gain early access to cutting-edge solutions, staying ahead of competitors.

Conclusion

While challenges such as high initial costs, infrastructure limitations, and regulatory complexities hinder the adoption of sustainable warehousing, these barriers are increasingly outweighed by opportunities for innovation, efficiency, and market leadership. As technology advances, consumer expectations evolve, and government support expands, warehouses have the potential to become central drivers of sustainability within the supply chain. By embracing these opportunities, warehousing operations can achieve the delicate balance of environmental stewardship, social responsibility, and economic growth, paving the way for a sustainable future.

Part II: Green Building Design and Construction

Sustainable Warehouse Design Principles

Warehousing forms the backbone of supply chain operations, yet its environmental footprint has long been a challenge. The demand for sustainable solutions has led to a focus on green building design and construction, integrating energy-efficient architecture and natural lighting and ventilation into warehouse designs. These principles not only reduce environmental impact but also enhance operational efficiency, create healthier work environments, and align with regulatory and market expectations. This chapter provides an analytical exploration of these principles, examining their benefits, implementation challenges, and role in fostering sustainable supply chains.

Energy-Efficient Architecture

Energy consumption in warehouses is significant, driven by lighting, heating, cooling, and machinery. Energy-efficient architecture aims to minimize this consumption through innovative design, material choice, and technology integration.

1. Structural Design for Energy Efficiency

The foundation of energy-efficient architecture lies in structural design, which determines the warehouse's overall energy profile.

Compact Designs: Reducing unnecessary space lowers heating, cooling, and lighting demands.

Thermal Performance: Insulated walls and roofs minimize energy loss, maintaining stable indoor temperatures and reducing HVAC loads.

Zoning: Segregating areas based on temperature requirements, such as cold storage or general inventory zones, prevents energy wastage in maintaining uniform conditions.

2. Use of Sustainable Materials

Material choice directly impacts the energy efficiency and sustainability of a warehouse.

Recycled Materials: Using recycled steel or concrete in construction reduces the energy footprint of material production.

High-Performance Glass: Double-glazed or low-emissivity glass minimizes heat gain or loss through windows, reducing HVAC demands.

Green Roofs: Vegetative roofing systems improve insulation, reduce urban heat island effects, and contribute to stormwater management.

Challenges:

Higher upfront costs for advanced materials can deter adoption.

Limited availability of certain sustainable materials in specific regions adds to logistical complexity.

3. Renewable Energy Integration

The incorporation of renewable energy sources is central to energy-efficient warehouse design.

Solar Panels: Photovoltaic systems on rooftops harness solar energy, reducing reliance on non-renewable power sources.

Geothermal Systems: Geothermal energy for heating and cooling offers a sustainable alternative to conventional HVAC systems.

Wind Energy: Where feasible, warehouses can integrate small-scale wind turbines to generate supplementary energy.

Analytical Insights:

The return on investment for renewable energy systems is long-term, with initial costs offset by lower utility bills and regulatory incentives such as tax credits or subsidies.

4. Advanced Insulation Techniques

Insulation plays a critical role in maintaining temperature stability within warehouses.

High-R-Value Materials: Using materials with high thermal resistance (R-value) ensures efficient temperature control.

Sealing and Weatherproofing: Preventing air leaks through doors, windows, and joints further enhances energy conservation.

Industry Example:

Amazon's energy-efficient warehouses incorporate advanced insulation and renewable energy systems, achieving LEED certification and significant energy savings.

5. Smart Energy Management

Technology integration optimizes energy use within energy-efficient architectural designs.

Building Management Systems (BMS): These systems monitor and control energy usage across lighting, HVAC, and machinery.

IoT Sensors: Real-time monitoring of energy-intensive operations allows for immediate adjustments to reduce waste.

Demand Response Systems: Warehouses can adapt energy usage based on peak and off-peak hours to save costs.

Challenges:

Integration with existing systems in older warehouses may be complex and expensive.

Ensuring data security within IoT-enabled systems is crucial to prevent operational disruptions.

Natural Lighting and Ventilation

The inclusion of natural lighting and ventilation systems in warehouse design enhances sustainability by reducing dependence on artificial lighting and mechanical ventilation systems. This dual strategy lowers energy consumption while improving the work environment.

1. Natural Lighting Strategies

Natural lighting, or daylighting, involves optimizing the use of sunlight within a warehouse.

Skylights and Clerestory Windows

Design Benefits: Strategically placed skylights and clerestory windows bring in abundant natural light without overheating the interior.

Energy Savings: Reduces dependence on artificial lighting during daylight hours, leading to lower electricity bills.

Light Shelves and Reflective Surfaces

Mechanism: Light shelves distribute daylight deeper into the interior, while reflective surfaces amplify its reach.

Applications: Particularly effective in large warehouses where light penetration is a challenge.

Challenges:

Potential glare and uneven light distribution need to be mitigated with appropriate window treatments.

Excessive heat gain from large skylights may increase cooling demands in hot climates.

2. Ventilation Systems

Natural ventilation systems replace or complement mechanical ventilation, using airflow dynamics to regulate indoor temperatures and air quality.

Cross-Ventilation

Mechanism: Placing vents or windows on opposite sides of the building allows air to flow naturally, creating a cooling effect.

Cost Efficiency: Eliminates or significantly reduces the need for mechanical cooling systems.

Stack Ventilation

Design: Incorporates high and low openings, leveraging temperature differences to move warm air out and draw cooler air in.

Sustainability Impact: Reduces reliance on energy-intensive HVAC systems.

Hybrid Systems

Combination of Natural and Mechanical Ventilation: Automatically switches between natural and mechanical systems based on external conditions.

Benefits: Balances energy savings with the need for consistent air quality.

3. Health and Productivity Benefits

Natural lighting and ventilation improve the indoor environment, directly influencing worker well-being and productivity.

Reduced Fatigue: Workers in naturally lit environments experience less eye strain and fatigue.

Enhanced Air Quality: Ventilation systems improve air circulation, reducing indoor pollutants and creating healthier conditions.

Increased Efficiency: Studies show that employees in well-lit and ventilated spaces are more productive and less prone to absenteeism.

Case Study:

A Walmart distribution center implementing natural lighting and ventilation reported a 10% increase in worker productivity and a 20% reduction in energy costs.

Integration of Energy Efficiency and Natural Design

The most sustainable warehouses combine energy-efficient architecture with natural lighting and ventilation for maximum impact.

Holistic Design Principles

Passive Solar Design: Aligning the warehouse's orientation to maximize sunlight in winter and minimize heat gain in summer.

Integrated Systems: Designing HVAC, lighting, and renewable energy systems to work cohesively enhances efficiency and reduces redundancies.

Lifecycle Analysis

Material Lifespan: Choosing durable materials reduces replacement needs and minimizes waste.

Operational Costs: Upfront investments in sustainable designs often result in lower long-term operational costs.

Economic and Environmental Impact

Cost-Benefit Analysis

Initial Investments: While sustainable designs involve higher costs, the long-term savings from reduced energy use often outweigh the initial expenses.

Tax Incentives and Subsidies: Governments and industry organizations provide financial support for warehouses adopting sustainable practices.

Environmental Contributions

Carbon Footprint Reduction: Energy-efficient and naturally ventilated warehouses significantly reduce greenhouse gas emissions.

Resource Conservation: Lower energy and material consumption aligns with global sustainability goals.

The principles of energy-efficient architecture and natural lighting and ventilation are central to designing sustainable warehouses. While challenges such as high initial costs and implementation complexities persist, the long-term economic and environmental benefits make these principles indispensable. As warehouses evolve to meet the demands of a green economy, adopting these sustainable design principles will not only enhance operational efficiency but also contribute to global sustainability efforts.

Energy-Efficient Construction Materials

Modern construction practices are increasingly oriented toward sustainability, particularly in warehouse design, where energy efficiency is a crucial concern. The use of energy-efficient construction materials has emerged as a cornerstone of sustainable building practices, helping to minimize environmental impact while optimizing operational costs. This chapter delves into the adoption of eco-friendly materials and green building technologies, exploring their properties, applications, and implications for energy-efficient warehouse construction.

Use of Eco-Friendly Materials

Eco-friendly materials are designed to reduce the environmental footprint of buildings while providing the durability and performance necessary for industrial applications like warehousing. These materials are sustainable because they are either renewable, recyclable, or have lower embodied energy.

1. Characteristics of Eco-Friendly Materials

Eco-friendly materials exhibit several defining characteristics that make them ideal for sustainable construction:

Low Embodied Energy: These materials consume minimal energy during production and transportation.

Renewability: Materials like bamboo and timber are renewable, making them a sustainable choice.

Recyclability: Metals, concrete, and certain plastics can be repurposed, extending their lifecycle.

Non-Toxicity: Materials that do not release harmful chemicals ensure better indoor air quality.

2. Common Eco-Friendly Materials for Warehousing

Several materials stand out for their energy-efficient and eco-friendly properties:

a. Recycled Steel

Recycled steel is widely used in warehouse construction due to its high strength-to-weight ratio and recyclability.

Properties: Steel retains its structural integrity even after recycling, reducing the demand for virgin materials.

Applications: Beams, columns, and roofing systems in warehouses frequently utilize recycled steel.

Environmental Impact: Reusing steel significantly reduces energy consumption compared to producing new steel.

b. Insulated Concrete Forms (ICFs)

ICFs are lightweight, modular concrete blocks with built-in insulation, making them an energy-efficient option.

Properties: They offer superior thermal insulation, reducing HVAC energy usage.

Applications: Walls and foundations benefit from the energy-saving properties of ICFs.

Environmental Impact: By improving energy efficiency, ICFs contribute to lower greenhouse gas emissions.

c. Bamboo

Bamboo is a renewable material with excellent tensile strength, increasingly utilized in sustainable building practices.

Properties: It grows rapidly, sequesters carbon dioxide, and is biodegradable.

Applications: Structural frameworks, flooring, and decorative elements often incorporate bamboo.

Environmental Impact: Bamboo's renewability and low carbon footprint make it a key material for sustainable design.

d. Low-Emission Glass

Low-emission (low-E) glass coatings minimize heat transfer, improving a warehouse's energy performance.

Properties: This glass reflects infrared radiation while allowing natural light to pass through.

Applications: Frequently used in skylights and windows, especially in warehouses prioritizing daylight utilization.

Environmental Impact: Reduced energy usage for heating and cooling offsets the environmental cost of glass production.

Green Building Technologies

The integration of green building technologies is transforming warehouse construction, emphasizing energy efficiency and sustainability. These technologies reduce energy consumption, enhance environmental performance, and support operational efficiency.

1. Insulation Technologies

Insulation plays a critical role in maintaining indoor temperatures, reducing energy requirements for heating and cooling.

a. Spray Foam Insulation

Spray foam expands to fill gaps and cracks, creating an airtight seal.

Properties: Excellent thermal resistance (R-value), preventing heat loss or gain.

Applications: Used in walls, roofs, and floors to optimize energy performance.

Environmental Impact: Reduces the overall energy demand of HVAC systems, minimizing carbon emissions.

b. Reflective Insulation

Reflective materials prevent heat absorption by reflecting radiant energy away from the building.

Properties: Ideal for hot climates, where cooling demand is high.

Applications: Frequently installed in roofing systems and wall panels.

Environmental Impact: Reduces dependency on air conditioning, lowering energy consumption.

2. Smart Building Systems

Technology integration is essential for monitoring and optimizing energy use in warehouses.

a. Energy Management Systems (EMS)

EMS integrates sensors and software to track and control energy usage.

Functionality: Enables real-time monitoring of lighting, HVAC, and equipment energy consumption.

Applications: Frequently installed in large warehouses to optimize energy efficiency.

Environmental Impact: Helps identify and eliminate energy waste, reducing the building's carbon footprint.

b. IoT-Based Solutions

The Internet of Things (IoT) enables interconnected devices to streamline energy usage.

Functionality: Sensors adjust lighting, heating, and ventilation based on occupancy and weather conditions.

Applications: Warehouses utilize IoT to automate energy-saving strategies.

Environmental Impact: Significant reductions in energy consumption contribute to lower operational emissions.

Advantages of Energy-Efficient Construction Materials and Technologies

1. Cost Savings

Energy-efficient materials and technologies lower utility costs, improving the economic viability of warehouses.

Lower Energy Bills: Insulation and efficient HVAC systems reduce heating and cooling costs.

Reduced Maintenance: Durable materials like ICFs and recycled steel minimize long-term maintenance expenses.

2. Improved Environmental Performance

These materials and technologies mitigate environmental impacts by conserving resources and reducing emissions.

Reduced Carbon Footprint: Lower energy consumption results in decreased greenhouse gas emissions.

Sustainable Resource Use: The reliance on recycled and renewable materials preserves natural resources.

3. Enhanced Regulatory Compliance

Energy-efficient designs align with sustainability regulations and certification standards.

Certifications: Materials and technologies often meet criteria for LEED and ISO certifications.

Market Advantage: Green-certified warehouses are more attractive to environmentally conscious clients.

Challenges in Implementation

Despite their benefits, the adoption of energy-efficient materials and technologies is not without challenges:

1. High Initial Costs

The upfront cost of eco-friendly materials and advanced technologies can be prohibitive.

Financial Barriers: Budget constraints may prevent smaller firms from adopting sustainable practices.

ROI Concerns: The payback period for these investments can be lengthy, discouraging stakeholders.

2. Supply Chain Limitations

The availability of certain materials and technologies is often limited, complicating procurement.

Material Scarcity: Regions lacking access to recycled or specialized materials face supply chain hurdles.

Logistical Complexity: Transporting materials like bamboo or ICFs from distant suppliers increases costs and emissions.

3. Knowledge and Expertise Gaps

Effective implementation requires specialized knowledge and skills.

Skill Shortages: Contractors may lack experience in installing and utilizing advanced materials or systems.

Training Needs: Investing in workforce training is essential but adds to upfront costs.

Case Studies in Energy-Efficient Warehousing

1. Amazon Fulfillment Center, Sacramento

Amazon's fulfillment center incorporates energy-efficient materials and green technologies.

Eco-Friendly Materials: Recycled steel and low-E glass enhance the building's sustainability.

Green Technologies: Solar panels and advanced insulation minimize energy consumption.

Outcome: The facility achieved LEED Gold certification, reducing its carbon footprint significantly.

2. Walmart Distribution Center, Alberta

Walmart's sustainable distribution center sets a benchmark for energy efficiency.

Insulation: The use of spray foam and reflective insulation improved energy performance.

Smart Systems: IoT-enabled energy management systems optimize operational efficiency.

Outcome: The warehouse operates at 60% lower energy consumption compared to conventional facilities.

Future Trends in Energy-Efficient Construction

Advances in technology and material science continue to shape the future of sustainable warehousing.

1. Nanomaterials

Nanotechnology is enabling the development of ultra-efficient insulation and structural materials.

Properties: Nanomaterials offer superior thermal resistance and durability.

Applications: Expected to revolutionize energy efficiency in roofing and wall systems.

2. Renewable Construction Materials

Innovations in renewable materials promise to make sustainable construction more accessible.

Examples: Hempcrete and bio-based plastics are gaining popularity for their environmental benefits.

3. Integrated Building Systems

The convergence of green technologies into unified systems will streamline energy optimization.

Applications: Smart grids integrated with warehouses will enable real-time energy adjustments.

Energy-efficient construction materials and green technologies are essential for creating sustainable warehouses. While challenges such as high initial costs and material availability persist, their long-term benefits for cost savings, environmental performance, and regulatory compliance are undeniable. As advancements continue, the integration of these materials and technologies will define the future of sustainable warehousing, balancing economic viability with environmental stewardship.

Renewable Energy Solutions in Warehousing

Warehousing operations are critical components of global supply chains but are also significant consumers of energy. Traditional energy sources used in warehouses, such as fossil fuels, contribute to greenhouse gas emissions and environmental degradation. Renewable energy solutions are revolutionizing warehouse management by offering sustainable, cost-effective, and environmentally friendly alternatives. This chapter explores the adoption of solar panels, wind turbines, and geothermal energy in warehousing and highlights case studies that demonstrate the practical applications and benefits of these technologies.

Solar Panels: Harnessing the Sun's Power

Solar energy is one of the most accessible and widely adopted renewable energy solutions for warehouses. Photovoltaic (PV) solar panels convert sunlight into electricity, providing a sustainable energy source for lighting, heating, cooling, and powering equipment.

1. Benefits of Solar Panels in Warehousing

Cost Savings: Solar energy significantly reduces utility bills by offsetting the need for grid electricity.

Energy Independence: Warehouses with solar installations can generate their own power, reducing dependency on external energy suppliers.

Environmental Impact: Solar energy produces no emissions during operation, making it a clean and sustainable option.

2. Applications in Warehouses

Rooftop Installations: Flat warehouse roofs provide an ideal surface for installing large arrays of solar panels.

Solar-Powered Lighting: Solar energy is used for indoor and outdoor lighting systems, enhancing energy efficiency.

Integrated Systems: Solar panels can be integrated with battery storage to provide power during cloudy days or at night.

3. Challenges in Implementation

Initial Costs: The installation of solar panels can be expensive, though subsidies and tax incentives often mitigate these costs.

Weather Dependence: Solar energy production is contingent on sunlight availability, which can vary by location and season.

Wind Turbines: Capturing Wind Energy

Wind turbines are another effective renewable energy solution for warehouses, particularly in regions with high wind speeds. By converting kinetic energy from the wind into electricity, wind turbines offer a complementary energy source to solar power.

1. Benefits of Wind Energy in Warehousing

High Efficiency: Modern wind turbines are highly efficient in converting wind into usable energy.

Scalability: Wind turbines can be scaled to meet the energy demands of small warehouses or large distribution centers.

Reduced Carbon Footprint: Wind energy is a zero-emission power source, aligning with sustainability goals.

2. Applications in Warehousing

On-Site Wind Turbines: Warehouses in windy locations can install turbines on-site to generate electricity for operations.

Hybrid Systems: Combining wind energy with solar panels creates a reliable energy mix, leveraging both sunny and windy conditions.

3. Challenges in Implementation

Space Requirements: Wind turbines require sufficient space for installation, which may not be available in urban or compact warehouse sites.

Noise and Visual Impact: Noise from turbines and their visual impact can pose challenges, especially in densely populated areas.

Geothermal Energy: Tapping into the Earth's Heat

Geothermal energy systems use heat from beneath the Earth's surface to provide sustainable heating and cooling solutions. This renewable energy source is particularly effective for temperature-controlled warehouses, such as those used for food storage or pharmaceuticals.

1. Benefits of Geothermal Energy in Warehousing

Energy Efficiency: Geothermal systems are highly efficient, requiring less energy to maintain consistent temperatures.

Cost Stability: Geothermal energy costs are not subject to the price volatility of fossil fuels.

Longevity: Geothermal systems have long operational lifespans, reducing maintenance and replacement costs.

2. Applications in Warehouses

HVAC Systems: Geothermal heat pumps provide efficient heating, cooling, and ventilation for warehouses.

Cold Storage: Geothermal energy maintains precise temperature controls in refrigerated and frozen storage facilities.

Hybrid Systems: Geothermal systems can complement solar or wind energy to meet varying energy demands.

3. Challenges in Implementation

High Initial Investment: Installing geothermal systems requires significant upfront costs, particularly for drilling and infrastructure.

Location-Specific: The feasibility of geothermal energy depends on local geological conditions, limiting its universal application.

Case Studies of Energy-Efficient Warehouses

1. Walmart's Sustainable Distribution Center, Alberta, Canada

Walmart's Alberta distribution center is a pioneering example of integrating renewable energy into warehousing.

Renewable Energy Features:

Solar panels cover the roof, generating a substantial portion of the warehouse's energy needs.

On-site wind turbines supplement the energy mix, particularly during the winter months.

A geothermal system regulates the building's heating and cooling requirements.

Outcomes:

The facility operates with 60% less energy compared to conventional warehouses.

It has achieved LEED Gold certification, underscoring its sustainability credentials.

2. Amazon Fulfillment Center, Sacramento, California

Amazon's Sacramento facility demonstrates how solar energy can drive energy-efficient warehouse operations.

Renewable Energy Features:

A rooftop solar array generates enough electricity to power lighting, HVAC systems, and conveyor belts.

Smart energy management systems optimize energy use and monitor performance.

Outcomes:

The center has reduced its annual energy consumption by 40%, significantly lowering its carbon footprint.

3. IKEA's Green Distribution Center, Italy

IKEA's Italian distribution center is a leader in renewable energy integration.

Renewable Energy Features:

Solar panels cover both the roof and parking areas, producing energy for warehouse operations and electric vehicle charging.

Wind turbines on-site provide additional electricity during peak demand periods.

Outcomes:

The center operates entirely on renewable energy, making it a zero-emission facility.

The Role of Renewable Energy in Sustainable Warehousing

Renewable energy solutions are transforming warehouses into energy-efficient, environmentally responsible facilities. By adopting solar panels, wind turbines, and geothermal systems, warehouses can achieve substantial cost savings, reduce their carbon footprints, and enhance their resilience to energy price fluctuations.

These technologies also contribute to broader sustainability goals by reducing reliance on non-renewable resources and aligning with regulatory standards for green building practices. While challenges such as high initial investments and site-specific limitations persist, the long-term benefits of renewable energy far outweigh these barriers.

As renewable energy technologies continue to evolve, their adoption in warehousing will become increasingly accessible and impactful, paving the way for a more sustainable future in supply chain management.

Part III: Optimizing Warehouse Operations

Energy Management in Warehouse Operations

Energy management is a critical aspect of warehouse operations, especially as businesses are increasingly under pressure to reduce operational costs and minimize their environmental impact. Warehouses are energy-intensive environments, with lighting, heating, cooling, ventilation, and machinery often consuming significant amounts of power. By implementing energy-efficient strategies, warehouses can not only reduce costs but also contribute to sustainability goals, improve their reputation, and comply with regulations. This chapter explores the key components of energy management in warehouse operations, including energy monitoring systems and strategies to reduce electricity and fuel consumption.

Energy Monitoring Systems

Energy monitoring systems (EMS) are sophisticated tools used to track, analyze, and optimize energy usage across warehouse facilities. These systems provide real-time data, allowing warehouse managers to identify energy consumption patterns, detect inefficiencies, and implement corrective actions. The goal of energy monitoring is to improve operational efficiency, reduce waste, and lower energy bills, all while minimizing the carbon footprint of the warehouse.

1. Components of Energy Monitoring Systems

Sensors and Meters: Energy monitoring systems use a variety of sensors and meters to capture data on energy consumption from different parts of the warehouse. These can include smart meters that track electricity, gas, and water usage, as well as specialized sensors that measure temperature, humidity, and air quality.

Data Analytics Platform: The collected data is sent to an analytics platform, which processes and analyzes the information. The platform generates reports, visualizes trends, and provides insights that help managers make data-driven decisions about energy usage.

Automation and Alerts: Modern EMS are often integrated with automation systems, allowing for real-time adjustments. For instance, if energy consumption spikes unexpectedly or exceeds a pre-set threshold, the system can automatically send alerts to facility managers or even adjust settings (such as dimming lights or reducing HVAC output) to optimize energy use.

2. Benefits of Energy Monitoring Systems

Real-Time Energy Insights: By continuously monitoring energy consumption, warehouse managers can identify energy-intensive processes and address inefficiencies promptly. For example, if certain machines or sections of the warehouse are consuming more energy than necessary, the EMS will highlight the issue.

Predictive Maintenance: Energy monitoring can also help predict when equipment is likely to fail due to energy inefficiencies, allowing for proactive maintenance. This reduces downtime and extends the lifespan of machinery.

Cost Savings: With detailed insights into energy consumption patterns, warehouses can implement targeted strategies to reduce usage, leading to significant cost savings over time.

Regulatory Compliance: Many regions have strict energy regulations, and energy management systems can help warehouses comply with energy efficiency standards and avoid penalties.

Reducing Electricity and Fuel Consumption

Reducing electricity and fuel consumption is central to optimizing energy use in warehouses. By taking a holistic approach that targets both operational processes and infrastructure, warehouses can reduce their environmental impact and improve energy efficiency.

1. Lighting Optimization

Lighting is one of the largest energy consumers in warehouses, as large facilities typically require extensive lighting systems to ensure proper visibility for workers and safety. Strategies to reduce lighting energy consumption include:

LED Lighting: Replacing conventional lighting with energy-efficient LED lights is one of the most effective ways to reduce electricity usage in warehouses. LED lights use up to 75% less energy than traditional incandescent bulbs and have a longer lifespan, reducing the frequency of replacements.

Motion Sensors and Timers: Installing motion sensors in areas that are not continuously in use (such as storage aisles, restrooms, and offices) ensures that lights are only on when needed. Timers and daylight sensors can also be used to adjust lighting levels based on the time of day or natural light availability, further reducing energy waste.

Zoning and Control Systems: Advanced lighting control systems allow for the zoning of different areas of the warehouse. For example, brighter lighting can be used in areas where workers are actively engaged, while dimmer lighting can be used in storage zones. This ensures that energy is not wasted in areas that do not require full illumination.

2. HVAC Optimization

Heating, ventilation, and air conditioning (HVAC) systems are another major energy consumer in warehouses, especially in climate-controlled facilities. Strategies for reducing HVAC energy consumption include:

Smart Thermostats and Controls: Installing smart thermostats that automatically adjust temperatures based on occupancy and external weather conditions can significantly reduce energy usage. For example, the HVAC system can be programmed to reduce heating or cooling in unoccupied areas of the warehouse or during non-peak hours.

Airflow Optimization: In large warehouses, ensuring that air circulation is optimized can reduce the workload on HVAC systems. Installing fans to move hot or cold air more efficiently can help maintain consistent temperatures with less energy. Additionally, insulating roofs and walls can help retain temperature control, reducing the energy required for heating and cooling.

Energy Recovery Systems: Some warehouses are adopting energy recovery systems that capture excess heat from industrial processes (such as refrigeration or machinery) and reuse it to heat the building. This reduces the need for additional heating from fossil-fuel-powered systems.

3. Material Handling Equipment (MHE)

Material handling equipment (MHE), such as forklifts, conveyors, and automated guided vehicles (AGVs), can also be significant energy consumers in warehouses. To reduce electricity and fuel consumption, warehouses can adopt the following strategies:

Electric Forklifts and AGVs: Transitioning from diesel or gas-powered forklifts to electric-powered equipment can lead to substantial energy savings. Electric MHE is not only more efficient but also eliminates fuel costs and reduces greenhouse gas emissions.

Regenerative Braking: Some modern MHE systems are equipped with regenerative braking, a technology that recaptures energy typically lost during braking and converts it back into electricity for use by the equipment.

Energy-Efficient Conveyors: Conveyors are often in continuous operation, consuming large amounts of electricity. Installing energy-efficient motors, optimizing conveyor speeds, and implementing advanced sensors for controlling operational cycles can reduce energy consumption.

4. Warehouse Layout and Workflow Design

Efficient warehouse layouts and optimized workflows can reduce the need for energy-intensive processes. Well-designed layouts reduce the distances that material handling equipment and workers need to travel, minimizing fuel and electricity consumption. Additionally, designing the warehouse to improve storage density and reduce the number of times items need to be moved can enhance operational efficiency and decrease the overall energy usage.

Cross-Docking: Cross-docking, which involves transferring goods directly from inbound to outbound transportation without long-term storage, reduces the need for storage space and the energy required to maintain that space.

Optimizing Picking Strategies: Using intelligent order picking strategies, such as batch picking or zone picking, can reduce the number of trips that workers or automated systems need to make to collect items, decreasing energy use in the process.

5. Renewable Energy Integration

Integrating renewable energy sources like solar panels or wind turbines can supplement the electricity needed to run warehouse operations. Solar panels on warehouse roofs can provide a significant portion of the energy required, reducing reliance on grid electricity and cutting overall energy costs.

Furthermore, integrating energy storage systems, such as batteries, can help warehouse operators store excess energy generated during the day for use at night or during peak demand periods.

6. Fleet Management and Fuel Optimization

For warehouses with delivery or transportation operations, reducing fuel consumption in fleet vehicles is essential. Strategies to optimize fuel usage include:

Telematics Systems: Telemetry systems allow warehouse managers to track fleet vehicle performance, monitor fuel efficiency, and detect instances of excessive idling or inefficient driving. These insights help optimize routes, reduce fuel consumption, and enhance fleet maintenance.

Electric or Hybrid Vehicles: Transitioning to electric or hybrid delivery vehicles can significantly reduce the fuel consumption associated with transportation and delivery operations.

Energy management in warehouse operations is not only a key factor in reducing costs but also in achieving sustainability objectives. By implementing energy monitoring systems, optimizing electricity usage, and adopting fuel-efficient technologies, warehouses can lower their energy consumption and reduce their environmental impact. The strategies outlined in this chapter provide a roadmap for warehouses to become more energy-efficient, demonstrating that sustainability and cost savings go hand-in-hand in today's competitive logistics environment. With the continuous advancements in energy-efficient technologies and renewable energy sources, warehouses can look forward to even greater efficiencies in the future.

Part III: Optimizing Warehouse Operations

Water Conservation in Warehouses

Water conservation is a critical component of sustainable warehouse management, particularly in areas where water scarcity is a concern or where there is a strong regulatory focus on resource conservation. Warehouses are typically large facilities that require substantial water for various operations, from cooling systems to employee restrooms and cleaning processes. Given the increasing global demand for water, coupled with rising environmental concerns, warehouses are exploring innovative methods to minimize water consumption. Implementing water-saving technologies not only reduces operational costs but also helps improve a warehouse's environmental footprint. This chapter explores two primary water conservation strategies in warehouses: rainwater harvesting systems and the use of low-flow fixtures and wastewater recycling.

Rainwater Harvesting Systems

Rainwater harvesting involves capturing and storing rainwater for use in non-potable applications, such as irrigation, cooling, and cleaning. This practice has gained traction across a wide range of industries, including warehousing, as businesses seek sustainable solutions to reduce their dependence on municipal water sources and lower water costs.

1. How Rainwater Harvesting Works

A rainwater harvesting system typically consists of a network of gutters, downspouts, storage tanks, and filtration units. Here's how the system works:

Collection: Rainwater is collected from the roof of the warehouse facility, where it is channeled through gutters and downspouts.

Filtration: Before being stored, the rainwater is filtered to remove debris, leaves, and other contaminants. This step ensures that the water is clean and safe for non-potable uses.

Storage: Once filtered, the rainwater is stored in large tanks or cisterns. These storage systems can be above-ground or underground, depending on space availability and the volume of water required.

Distribution: The stored rainwater can be pumped into the facility's plumbing system to be used for irrigation, cooling systems, cleaning, or even for flushing toilets in restrooms.

2. Benefits of Rainwater Harvesting

Cost Savings: By reducing the reliance on municipal water supply, warehouses can lower their water bills. This is especially beneficial in areas where water is expensive or subject to rising rates.

Sustainability: Using rainwater reduces the demand for freshwater resources, making it an eco-friendly option for warehouses looking to decrease their environmental impact. The practice of rainwater harvesting also contributes to stormwater management by reducing runoff and helping prevent flooding.

Emergency Backup: In case of disruptions to the municipal water supply due to droughts or infrastructure issues, rainwater harvesting can provide a reliable source of water for essential operations.

Regulatory Compliance: In many regions, regulations and incentives encourage water conservation. Implementing rainwater harvesting systems can help warehouses meet sustainability goals and qualify for government rebates or tax credits.

3. Applications of Harvested Rainwater in Warehouses

Landscape Irrigation: Rainwater can be used to water green spaces around the warehouse, reducing the need for potable water for landscaping.

Cooling Systems: Some warehouses rely on evaporative cooling systems to regulate temperatures. Rainwater can be used in place of potable water in these cooling systems, reducing water consumption in large facilities.

Cleaning: Rainwater can be used for cleaning equipment, floors, and other areas of the warehouse that do not require potable water. This reduces reliance on municipal water supplies for everyday cleaning tasks.

Toilet Flushing: Harvested rainwater can be plumbed into the building's restroom facilities, where it can be used for flushing toilets and urinals. This significantly lowers water consumption for non-potable uses.

4. Design Considerations for Rainwater Harvesting Systems

When installing a rainwater harvesting system in a warehouse, several factors must be considered to ensure its effectiveness:

Roof Area: The size of the roof determines the amount of rainwater that can be collected. Larger roofs provide more surface area for water collection, which translates into higher storage capacity.

Storage Capacity: The size of the storage tanks must be adequate to meet the warehouse's water needs, particularly during dry spells when rainfall may be minimal.

Filtration Systems: Effective filtration is crucial to ensure that the collected rainwater is free from contaminants and debris.

Filtration systems should be regularly maintained to keep the water clean and safe.

Climate Conditions: The feasibility of rainwater harvesting depends on the climate and rainfall patterns of the region. In areas with frequent rain, harvesting can provide a substantial water supply. However, in drier climates, it may be necessary to supplement with other water-saving strategies.

Low-Flow Fixtures and Recycling Wastewater

Beyond rainwater harvesting, warehouses can also adopt water-saving technologies such as low-flow fixtures and wastewater recycling systems. These solutions not only reduce water consumption but also improve the overall efficiency of warehouse operations.

1. Low-Flow Fixtures

Low-flow fixtures are plumbing devices designed to reduce the amount of water used for various tasks, such as washing hands, flushing toilets, and cleaning floors. By restricting the flow of water, these fixtures help reduce overall consumption without compromising functionality.

Low-Flow Toilets: Traditional toilets use between 3.5 to 7 gallons of water per flush, whereas low-flow toilets use only 1.6 gallons or less. This can result in substantial water savings, particularly in large warehouses with multiple restroom facilities.

Low-Flow Faucets: Low-flow faucets and aerators are designed to reduce the flow rate of water while maintaining sufficient pressure for tasks like handwashing. These fixtures typically use less than 2.5 gallons per minute (GPM), significantly reducing water waste.

Low-Flow Showers: If the warehouse provides shower facilities for employees, low-flow showerheads can reduce water consumption by 30-50% compared to traditional fixtures.

Low-Flow Urinals: Similar to low-flow toilets, water-efficient urinals use significantly less water per flush. Some models even utilize no water at all, using air pressure or other methods to remove waste.

2. Benefits of Low-Flow Fixtures

Immediate Water Savings: Installing low-flow fixtures can immediately reduce water usage in the warehouse, translating into cost savings on water bills.

Low Maintenance: These fixtures require little maintenance while continuing to perform their functions effectively, making them a cost-efficient option for water conservation.

Regulatory Compliance: In many regions, water conservation regulations require the use of low-flow fixtures in commercial buildings. By adopting these fixtures, warehouses ensure compliance with local regulations and avoid penalties.

3. Wastewater Recycling

Wastewater recycling involves the treatment and reuse of water from various warehouse activities, such as cleaning, washing, and cooling. Instead of being discarded into the sewage system, the wastewater is filtered, treated, and returned to the system for reuse in other applications.

Greywater Recycling: Greywater is non-potable water that comes from sources such as sinks, showers, and laundry. By installing greywater recycling systems, warehouses can reuse this water for tasks like landscaping or toilet flushing.

Closed-Loop Systems: In some warehouses, a closed-loop water recycling system can be installed to reuse water in cooling systems, cleaning, and even some manufacturing processes. This system collects and filters water multiple times, reducing the need for fresh water from external sources.

Water Treatment Systems: To ensure that wastewater is safe for reuse, advanced treatment technologies such as filtration, ultraviolet (UV) disinfection, and reverse osmosis can be implemented to purify the water before it is reused.

4. Benefits of Wastewater Recycling

Reduced Freshwater Demand: Wastewater recycling reduces the demand for freshwater from external sources, helping conserve water resources and lower water utility costs.

Compliance with Environmental Regulations: In many regions, wastewater recycling is part of broader environmental regulations that encourage or mandate water reuse for non-potable purposes.

Environmental Impact Reduction: By recycling wastewater, warehouses can significantly reduce their environmental footprint, contributing to sustainable water management practices.

Conclusion

Water conservation is a vital aspect of sustainable warehouse operations. By implementing rainwater harvesting systems and utilizing low-flow fixtures and wastewater recycling technologies, warehouses can significantly reduce their water consumption, lower operational costs, and contribute to broader sustainability goals. As businesses continue to face pressure to adopt eco-friendly practices, water conservation represents an opportunity for warehouses to minimize their environmental impact while improving operational efficiency. The integration of these water-saving technologies not only aligns with corporate sustainability objectives but also provides warehouses with a competitive advantage by reducing costs and enhancing their green credentials.

Waste Management in Warehousing

Waste management plays a pivotal role in sustainable warehouse operations. As warehouses deal with a variety of materials—ranging from inventory goods to packaging materials—effectively managing waste is crucial for reducing environmental impact and promoting resource efficiency. Sustainable waste management in warehousing involves the strategies of reducing, reusing, and recycling waste. By adopting these practices, warehouses can lower their carbon footprint, minimize landfill contributions, and adhere to environmental regulations, all while fostering a more eco-friendly, cost-effective operation.

This chapter delves into the critical components of waste management in warehousing, focusing on the reduction of waste generation, the reuse of materials, and the recycling of waste products. Furthermore, it explores the management of packaging materials in a sustainable manner, which has become a major concern in logistics and warehousing due to the vast amounts of packaging waste generated by e-commerce and global supply chains.

Reducing, Reusing, and Recycling Waste in Warehousing

The "3 Rs" of waste management—Reduce, Reuse, and Recycle—form the foundation of a sustainable approach to waste management in warehouses. These principles aim to minimize waste generation, optimize the use of resources, and promote the responsible disposal of materials that cannot be reused. Let's take a closer look at each principle and how it applies to warehouse operations.

1. Reducing Waste Generation

The first step in sustainable waste management is reducing the amount of waste produced. By focusing on waste reduction, warehouses can avoid unnecessary costs and minimize their environmental impact from the outset.

Optimizing Inventory Management: Efficient inventory management practices such as Just-In-Time (JIT) or lean inventory systems can significantly reduce waste. JIT helps warehouses to align production schedules with actual demand, preventing overstocking and reducing waste associated with expired, obsolete, or damaged goods. This, in turn, minimizes the quantity of products that need to be discarded due to spoilage or excess.

Process Efficiency: Streamlining warehouse operations can help reduce waste generation. This includes reducing material handling errors, improving the design of processes to minimize wastage, and enhancing the precision of inventory forecasting. By focusing on these efficiency improvements, warehouses can prevent the overuse of materials and minimize the disposal of defective or excess inventory.

Packaging Waste Minimization: Packaging materials such as plastic wraps, cardboard boxes, and Styrofoam can generate significant waste. By adopting packaging designs that use fewer materials or opting for alternative, more sustainable packaging options, warehouses can reduce the overall volume of waste generated. Packaging that is over-engineered or unnecessarily large should be eliminated in favor of more optimized, space-efficient designs.

Energy and Resource Efficiency: Energy and water conservation efforts also contribute to waste reduction. Reducing energy use in heating, cooling, and lighting, as well as implementing more efficient systems for water use and heating, can reduce the overall waste output of a warehouse, including emissions and runoff.

2. Reusing Materials

The second principle in sustainable waste management is the reuse of materials. Reusing materials within the warehouse environment allows businesses to extend the life cycle of products, reducing the need for new materials and lowering overall waste output.

Reusable Packaging: One of the most effective ways warehouses can reuse materials is by using packaging that can be used multiple times. For example, durable plastic crates, wooden pallets, and metal containers can be reused for shipping goods multiple times. By investing in such reusable packaging solutions, warehouses can drastically reduce their need for disposable packaging and cut down on waste.

Returnable Shipping Containers: In certain warehouse settings, returnable or reusable shipping containers can be a significant waste-reducing solution. These containers are used for the transportation of goods and returned for reuse, which lowers the need for single-use shipping materials. By implementing a returnable container program, warehouses can reduce both packaging waste and transportation costs.

Reusing Pallets: Wooden pallets are commonly used in warehousing for stacking and moving inventory. Rather than discarding broken or damaged pallets, warehouses can repair and reuse them or repurpose them for other warehouse functions, such as creating temporary storage platforms or employee workstations. Pallet pooling systems, where pallets are exchanged among different organizations, are also an effective reuse strategy.

Office Supplies and Equipment: In warehouses, it is common for office supplies, equipment, and furniture to accumulate. Reusing office materials—such as repurposing old files, equipment, or furniture—can significantly cut down on office waste, contributing to a sustainable warehouse operation.

3. Recycling Waste Products

Recycling is a crucial component of any sustainable waste management strategy. It involves collecting materials that are no longer useful and processing them into raw materials that can be reused in production. By recycling waste products, warehouses can reduce the amount of material that ends up in landfills, conserving natural resources and reducing pollution.

Paper and Cardboard: Paper and cardboard waste is prevalent in warehouses, especially with regard to packaging materials. Recycled paper products are often in demand, so warehouses can sort and separate cardboard boxes, paper packaging, and other paper materials for collection by recycling companies. This practice helps conserve trees, reduces landfill use, and supports the recycling economy.

Plastic Recycling: Plastics, such as stretch film or shrink-wrap, are commonly used for packaging and palletizing products in warehouses. These materials can be difficult to recycle due to contamination and the complex nature of plastic polymers. However, more warehouses are investing in dedicated plastic recycling systems to collect and process these materials. Using specialized plastic recycling containers and partnering with local recycling firms can help ensure that plastic waste is properly handled.

Electronic Waste Recycling: As warehouses become more reliant on technology, the amount of electronic waste (e-waste) generated also increases. This includes old computers, printers, and other electronic devices. E-waste should be recycled through certified recycling programs to ensure that hazardous materials like heavy metals are safely disposed of and valuable components are recovered for reuse.

Metals and Glass: Metals such as aluminum, steel, and copper, as well as glass containers, can be recycled and used in a variety of applications. Warehouses that deal with these materials can establish designated recycling streams for metal and glass, contributing to a circular economy.

Managing Packaging Materials Sustainably

The packaging industry, including warehousing operations, is a significant contributor to waste production globally. Packaging materials, whether for shipping, storage, or protection, often end up in landfills, making sustainable packaging management a priority for warehouses aiming to reduce their environmental footprint.

1. Sustainable Packaging Design

Sustainable packaging is a core part of reducing waste in warehousing. The aim is to design packaging that uses fewer resources, is more efficient, and can be recycled or reused. Some key approaches to sustainable packaging design include:

Minimalist Packaging: Designing packaging that uses the least material while still protecting the product is essential. Packaging should be strong enough to ensure the safe delivery of goods but not over-engineered. For instance, using thinner cardboard, reducing unnecessary padding, or using molded pulp instead of Styrofoam can reduce waste without compromising product safety.

Use of Biodegradable Materials: Where possible, warehouses can replace plastic packaging materials with biodegradable alternatives. Materials such as biodegradable wraps, plant-based plastics, or recyclable packing peanuts made from cornstarch are excellent eco-friendly options.

Modular Packaging: Modular packaging involves creating packaging that fits multiple products or items into the same package, thus reducing the need for multiple separate packages. This strategy reduces material use and minimizes packaging waste.

Standardized Packaging: Standardizing packaging for different products helps minimize the variety of materials used, reducing complexity and waste. By using standard box sizes and materials, warehouses can more easily optimize storage and transportation while reducing packaging waste.

2. Packaging Material Recycling Programs

Managing packaging waste involves more than just sustainable design—it also includes an effective recycling program. Warehouses should establish recycling systems for cardboard, plastic, and other materials to ensure that packaging waste is diverted from landfills.

Collaboration with Suppliers: Warehouses can work with suppliers to encourage the use of packaging materials that are easy to recycle and require fewer resources. Collaborating with suppliers for packaging take-back programs is one way to create a more sustainable supply chain.

Consumer Incentives: Some warehouses, especially in the e-commerce sector, can encourage consumers to return or reuse packaging. This could include offering discounts for returns of packaging or incentivizing the return of reusable shipping containers.

On-Site Recycling Facilities: Large warehouses may benefit from on-site recycling facilities where employees can separate and prepare packaging materials for recycling. Installing recycling bins throughout the warehouse for paper, plastic, and metal can make it easier to manage waste and ensure proper disposal.

Waste management in warehouses is a multifaceted challenge that requires the concerted effort of all stakeholders—from warehouse operators to suppliers and consumers. By focusing on the "3 Rs" (reduce, reuse, and recycle), warehouses can reduce their environmental footprint, enhance operational efficiency, and contribute to the broader goals of sustainability. Additionally, sustainable packaging management practices play a critical role in reducing waste and improving warehouse sustainability. Adopting these practices not only aligns with environmental regulations but also improves brand reputation, reduces costs, and helps businesses thrive in an increasingly eco-conscious marketplace.

Efficient Material Handling and Storage

Efficient material handling and storage are essential components of warehouse operations. Proper handling ensures that goods are stored, moved, and retrieved in the most effective manner, reducing costs and increasing throughput. In a sustainable warehousing context, this efficiency extends beyond operations to encompass environmental responsibility. Sustainable material handling equipment, minimizing product damage, and reducing waste play critical roles in optimizing warehouse performance while minimizing the environmental impact.

This chapter focuses on the key components of efficient material handling and storage, specifically in the context of sustainability. It covers the adoption of sustainable material handling equipment, strategies for reducing product damage and wastage, and how these approaches contribute to the overall efficiency and sustainability of warehouse operations.

Sustainable Material Handling Equipment

Material handling equipment (MHE) includes all the devices and machinery used to move, store, control, and protect products in a warehouse or distribution center. Selecting and utilizing sustainable MHE is crucial to reducing the carbon footprint of warehouse operations. Below, we examine some of the leading sustainable material handling equipment options available today and their implications for warehouse efficiency and sustainability.

1. Electric Forklifts and Automated Guided Vehicles (AGVs)

Traditional internal combustion engine (ICE) forklifts contribute significantly to warehouse emissions, primarily due to their fuel consumption. However, electric forklifts and

AGVs are rapidly gaining popularity as more sustainable alternatives. These electric-powered solutions reduce reliance on fossil fuels, cut emissions, and lower energy consumption.

Electric Forklifts: Unlike their gas-powered counterparts, electric forklifts run on rechargeable batteries, significantly reducing carbon emissions and improving energy efficiency. They are especially beneficial in indoor environments, where air quality is crucial. While the initial investment can be higher than traditional forklifts, the long-term savings in energy costs and lower maintenance requirements make electric forklifts a cost-effective option in the long run.

Automated Guided Vehicles (AGVs): AGVs are increasingly used to automate material handling within warehouses. These vehicles can transport goods efficiently without the need for human intervention, reducing the chances of accidents, human error, and product damage. Many AGVs are powered by lithium-ion batteries, which are more efficient and longer-lasting than traditional lead-acid batteries. Furthermore, AGVs can work around the clock without breaks, leading to higher operational efficiency and the reduced need for additional machinery or staff.

2. Solar-Powered Material Handling Systems

Integrating renewable energy into material handling operations is a growing trend in sustainable warehouse management. Solar-powered material handling systems, such as solar-powered conveyors or cranes, harness sunlight to provide energy for warehouse operations. This reduces the warehouse's dependency on the grid, minimizing its carbon footprint.

Solar-Powered Conveyors: Conveyor systems are commonly used in warehouses to transport goods across different areas. By incorporating solar panels into the conveyor design, warehouses can reduce their energy consumption and increase the efficiency of their material handling operations. These systems work by generating electricity through solar power, which can directly power the conveyor or be stored for later use.

Solar Cranes: Solar-powered cranes, which are commonly used in loading and unloading shipments, are another example of sustainable material handling equipment. These cranes can be equipped with solar panels to charge their batteries, ensuring that the equipment remains operational while reducing greenhouse gas emissions.

3. Ergonomically Designed Equipment

Sustainability in material handling is not only about reducing environmental impact but also about promoting the well-being of warehouse workers. Ergonomically designed equipment that minimizes strain on workers can contribute to a safer, healthier, and more productive warehouse environment. By preventing repetitive strain injuries and reducing workplace accidents, ergonomically designed equipment also reduces the long-term costs associated with worker compensation and absenteeism.

Ergonomic Lifts and Pallet Jacks: Equipment designed to reduce physical strain on workers, such as ergonomic lifts and pallet jacks, can improve efficiency by enabling faster and safer handling of goods. These tools often use hydraulic systems that reduce the need for manual lifting, thereby reducing the risk of injury.

Automated Storage and Retrieval Systems (AS/RS): AS/RS are systems that automatically store and retrieve goods without human intervention. These systems help minimize the physical labor required by warehouse workers and reduce the risk of injury. By automating tasks that involve heavy lifting, warehouses can improve efficiency and safety while decreasing energy consumption and reducing environmental impact.

Reducing Product Damage and Wastage

Another essential aspect of efficient material handling and storage is minimizing product damage and wastage. Wastage not only leads to financial losses but also contributes to the overall inefficiency of warehouse operations. Implementing best practices for reducing damage during handling, storage, and transportation is key to improving both operational performance and sustainability.

1. Proper Storage Techniques

The manner in which products are stored in the warehouse plays a significant role in preventing damage and reducing wastage. Proper storage techniques ensure that goods are not subjected to physical stress, contamination, or environmental factors that could degrade their quality.

Temperature and Humidity Control: For certain types of goods, particularly perishable items or sensitive electronics, temperature and humidity control are crucial. Warehouses can implement temperature-controlled storage areas or use smart sensors that monitor and maintain optimal conditions for specific goods. This helps preserve product quality and reduce spoilage.

Racking Systems: The use of optimized racking systems is essential to reducing damage and wastage. Well-designed racking systems that securely hold items reduce the chances of items falling, getting crushed, or being otherwise damaged during handling. By carefully considering the weight, size, and fragility of products, warehouses can design custom racking solutions that cater to their specific needs.

Palletizing and Secure Loading: Palletizing is an essential technique for efficient material handling, as it ensures that products are stacked in a stable and organized manner. Properly secured pallets prevent items from shifting during transport, which reduces the risk of product damage. Additionally, using proper tie-downs and load-securing systems during transportation further minimizes the risk of wastage.

2. Employee Training and Best Practices

Employee training is vital to reducing product damage. Properly trained employees who are familiar with the correct handling techniques and safety protocols can prevent accidents that lead to product breakage, spoilage, or contamination.

Handling Fragile Items: Certain products, such as glassware or electronics, require special care during handling. Providing specific training for these items ensures that employees understand the necessary precautions. For example, fragile items should be handled with extra care and may require additional padding during transport.

Use of Proper Equipment: Ensuring that employees use the right material handling equipment for the job is critical to reducing damage. For example, using forklifts with adjustable forks, which can accommodate different pallet sizes, prevents damage during the loading and unloading process.

Regular Audits and Inspections: Conducting regular audits of material handling processes allows warehouses to identify potential issues that could lead to product damage. Inspections of pallets, storage areas, and handling equipment can ensure that everything is in optimal condition, reducing the risk of damage due to equipment failure or poor storage practices.

3. Packaging Improvements

Packaging plays an essential role in protecting products during handling and storage. Improved packaging techniques, such as the use of better materials or more robust packaging designs, can reduce the likelihood of damage and wastage.

Impact-Resistant Materials: Using packaging materials that are impact-resistant, such as bubble wrap, foam padding, or specialized cushioning materials, helps prevent products from being damaged during transportation and storage. These materials absorb shocks and protect fragile items.

Intelligent Packaging: In the era of Industry 4.0, intelligent packaging solutions are becoming more widespread. For example, packaging that incorporates RFID tags or QR codes can provide real-time tracking of products. This technology helps reduce the chances of misplacement, improves inventory accuracy, and reduces the risk of product damage due to mismanagement.

Efficient material handling and storage are fundamental to the success of a warehouse operation. By adopting sustainable material handling equipment, warehouses can reduce their environmental impact while improving operational efficiency. Additionally, focusing on proper storage techniques, employee training, and packaging improvements helps minimize product damage and wastage, which ultimately leads to greater sustainability and cost savings.

As sustainability continues to be a key driver in warehouse operations, the integration of sustainable material handling solutions and the implementation of best practices in storage and handling will be essential to achieving long-term success. By adopting these strategies, warehouses not only reduce their environmental footprint but also create a safer, more efficient, and cost-effective operation that supports the growth of sustainable supply chains.

Part IV: Technology for Sustainable Warehousing

Role of Automation and IoT in Sustainability

In recent years, automation and the Internet of Things (IoT) have become integral to improving operational efficiency and sustainability in warehousing. These technological advancements not only streamline processes but also contribute significantly to reducing energy consumption, minimizing waste, and enhancing overall resource management. As warehouses and distribution centers evolve, the combination of automation and IoT provides the tools necessary for businesses to meet the growing demands of sustainability while maintaining or increasing operational productivity.

This chapter delves into the role of automation and IoT in sustainable warehousing, with a specific focus on energy-efficient robots and conveyor systems, and how IoT can be leveraged to track and optimize resources in the warehouse environment.

Energy-Efficient Robots and Conveyor Systems

Automation has revolutionized the material handling processes in warehouses, enabling businesses to improve their operations while lowering energy consumption and environmental impact. The deployment of energy-efficient robots and conveyor systems is a central element in creating sustainable warehouses. These technologies not only enhance productivity but also reduce the warehouse's carbon footprint and improve the overall efficiency of the supply chain.

1. Energy-Efficient Robots

Robots in warehouses have advanced significantly in recent years, transitioning from simple, repetitive tasks to more sophisticated operations such as picking, packing, and sorting.

These robots are designed to operate with high efficiency and minimal energy consumption, contributing to overall energy savings in warehouse operations.

Automated Guided Vehicles (AGVs): One of the most common types of robots used in warehouses is the Automated Guided Vehicle (AGV). These battery-powered vehicles are used to move goods across the warehouse floor, replacing human labor and traditional forklifts. AGVs are equipped with sensors, cameras, and GPS systems to navigate the warehouse autonomously, improving efficiency while reducing the energy required to move items.

Collaborative Robots (Cobots): Cobots work alongside human employees, automating repetitive or physically demanding tasks. These robots are designed to complement human labor, reducing the workload for employees and enhancing overall productivity. By integrating advanced sensors and low-energy components, cobots help reduce energy consumption compared to traditional manual labor or more energy-intensive industrial robots.

Robotic Arms and Pick-and-Place Systems: Robotic arms equipped with grippers or suction cups are increasingly being used for picking and placing items in warehouses. These robots can operate with remarkable precision and speed, ensuring that goods are handled efficiently and with minimal energy consumption. Advanced robotic arms are often designed with energy-saving modes that enable them to reduce power usage when idle or in less demanding tasks.

2. Energy-Efficient Conveyor Systems

Conveyor systems are another staple in warehouse automation. They facilitate the efficient movement of goods between different warehouse sections, increasing throughput and reducing the need for human labor. To make these systems more energy-efficient, innovative technologies and design strategies are being employed.

Variable Frequency Drives (VFDs): VFDs allow conveyor motors to operate at different speeds based on demand, thereby reducing energy consumption. Instead of running at a constant speed, which can waste energy during low-demand periods, conveyors with VFDs adjust their operation according to the volume of goods being transported, ensuring optimal energy use.

Gravity-Powered Conveyors: Gravity-powered conveyors are another energy-efficient option for material handling. These systems rely on the force of gravity to move products along inclined tracks, eliminating the need for motors and reducing electricity consumption. Gravity conveyors are often used for sorting or accumulating goods, especially in areas with high throughput.

Low-Power Conveyor Motors: Advances in motor technology have led to the development of low-power, high-efficiency motors for conveyor systems. These motors are designed to use less electricity while delivering the same level of performance, reducing the warehouse's overall energy consumption.

Smart Conveyor Systems: Modern conveyor systems can be equipped with smart sensors and control systems that monitor and adjust operations in real-time. By optimizing the flow of goods and reducing unnecessary motion, these smart systems help to minimize the energy consumed in the process. They also provide valuable data for further energy optimization, helping warehouses to pinpoint areas where energy consumption can be reduced.

IoT for Tracking and Optimizing Resources

The Internet of Things (IoT) plays a transformative role in enhancing the sustainability of warehouse operations. By connecting physical objects—such as machines, sensors, and equipment—to the internet, IoT enables warehouses to collect and analyze real-time data, optimizing the use of resources and improving energy efficiency. The integration of IoT into warehousing systems facilitates better decision-making, resource management, and process optimization, making it a key tool for achieving sustainability goals.

1. Real-Time Tracking of Resources

IoT devices embedded in equipment, products, and infrastructure allow for continuous tracking of various resources in the warehouse. These smart sensors can monitor inventory levels, track the movement of goods, and assess the condition of materials, all of which contribute to optimizing warehouse operations.

Inventory Management: IoT-enabled inventory management systems provide real-time data about stock levels and product movement. By integrating RFID tags or barcodes with IoT technology, warehouse managers can accurately track products throughout the supply chain. This reduces the chances of overstocking or stockouts, leading to more efficient inventory management and less waste.

Asset Tracking: By embedding IoT sensors in assets such as pallets, racks, and equipment, warehouses can track the location, usage, and condition of each item. This provides valuable insights into asset utilization and helps prevent loss or misuse, leading to more efficient operations and longer equipment lifespans.

2. Optimizing Energy Consumption

IoT enables warehouses to collect data on energy usage across various operations, such as lighting, heating, cooling, and machinery. By monitoring energy consumption in real-time, warehouse operators can identify inefficiencies and take corrective action to reduce energy waste.

Smart Lighting Systems: IoT-connected lighting systems are a key example of how technology can optimize energy consumption. Smart lighting adjusts the brightness based on factors such as occupancy, time of day, and natural light levels. This ensures that lights are only on when necessary, reducing electricity usage and contributing to sustainability efforts.

Climate Control Systems: IoT-enabled climate control systems help maintain optimal temperature and humidity levels in warehouses. These systems automatically adjust heating and cooling based on real-time data, ensuring that energy is used efficiently without over-conditioning the environment. For example, IoT sensors can detect when an area of the warehouse is empty and reduce heating or cooling accordingly.

Energy Management Platforms: Energy management platforms integrated with IoT devices offer detailed insights into energy consumption patterns throughout the warehouse. By analyzing this data, warehouse managers can identify peak energy usage times, areas with high consumption, and opportunities for energy savings. These platforms can also automate energy-saving actions, such as adjusting temperature settings or switching off idle equipment.

3. Predictive Maintenance

IoT sensors can monitor the performance of critical warehouse equipment, such as forklifts, conveyors, and HVAC systems. These sensors detect early signs of wear and tear or potential malfunctions, enabling predictive maintenance that reduces downtime and prevents equipment failures.

Equipment Health Monitoring: By continuously tracking the performance and condition of machinery, IoT sensors provide data that can predict when maintenance is required. This approach ensures that maintenance is performed proactively, reducing the need for emergency repairs that can disrupt warehouse operations and lead to excessive energy consumption due to inefficient equipment.

Optimizing Equipment Lifespan: IoT-powered predictive maintenance can also extend the lifespan of warehouse equipment by ensuring it is always running at peak performance. Well-maintained machines consume less energy and operate more efficiently, contributing to overall sustainability goals.

The role of automation and IoT in sustainable warehousing cannot be overstated. Automation technologies such as energy-efficient robots and conveyor systems have revolutionized material handling, improving both operational efficiency and energy consumption. By incorporating IoT, warehouses can optimize resource usage, track assets in real-time, and enhance energy efficiency across the facility.

Through the combination of these advanced technologies, warehouses can not only meet their sustainability goals but also improve overall productivity, reduce waste, and lower operational costs. The ongoing advancements in automation and IoT offer tremendous potential for the future of sustainable warehousing, enabling businesses to remain competitive while contributing to a greener and more efficient supply chain.

Big Data and Analytics for Green Warehousing

As sustainability becomes an essential aspect of modern business practices, warehouses are increasingly leveraging big data and analytics to reduce their environmental impact. In the context of green warehousing, big data enables better decision-making that leads to more efficient operations, energy conservation, waste reduction, and the overall optimization of resources. By harnessing the power of predictive analytics and real-time data, warehouses can significantly improve their sustainability efforts while simultaneously reducing costs and improving productivity.

In this chapter, we will explore how big data and analytics are revolutionizing green warehousing, with a particular focus on predictive analytics for energy and waste reduction and optimizing inventory levels to avoid overstocking.

Predictive Analytics for Energy and Waste Reduction

Predictive analytics refers to the use of historical data, statistical algorithms, and machine learning techniques to predict future outcomes. In warehousing, predictive analytics helps companies anticipate energy usage patterns, reduce waste, and optimize resource allocation. By analyzing large volumes of data from IoT sensors, equipment, and historical usage, warehouses can forecast energy demand and identify areas where inefficiencies may occur, allowing for proactive adjustments.

1. Energy Consumption Forecasting

One of the primary ways predictive analytics contributes to green warehousing is by optimizing energy consumption.

Energy use in warehouses is typically high due to lighting, HVAC systems, and material handling equipment. However, by utilizing predictive models, warehouses can forecast energy usage patterns and reduce their carbon footprint.

Dynamic Energy Management: Predictive analytics can anticipate periods of high energy demand, such as during peak operational hours, and adjust energy consumption accordingly. For instance, based on historical data, the system can predict when energy consumption will peak (e.g., during product sorting or unloading). This allows warehouse managers to schedule energy-intensive operations during off-peak hours, reducing the overall demand on the energy grid and decreasing costs.

HVAC Optimization: Heating, ventilation, and air conditioning (HVAC) systems consume a significant amount of energy in warehouses, particularly in regions with extreme temperatures. Predictive analytics can analyze historical data on external weather patterns, internal temperatures, and warehouse activities to forecast when heating or cooling will be needed. This helps adjust HVAC systems proactively to maintain an optimal environment without unnecessary energy consumption.

Smart Lighting Systems: Predictive analytics can also optimize lighting systems in warehouses by analyzing foot traffic patterns and identifying areas that require lighting at specific times of the day. For instance, in areas with minimal activity, lighting can be reduced or turned off automatically, while areas with high activity can have lighting levels adjusted dynamically. By analyzing patterns, the system can ensure that energy is only used when necessary, which can lead to significant energy savings.

2. Waste Reduction through Predictive Models

Warehouses generate significant amounts of waste, ranging from packaging materials to unsold products. Predictive analytics plays a critical role in waste reduction by anticipating potential waste sources and identifying areas where excess materials or products may be generated.

Optimizing Packaging Usage: One of the largest sources of waste in warehousing comes from packaging materials. Predictive analytics can forecast packaging requirements based on order history, seasonal fluctuations, and specific product characteristics. By predicting the amount of packaging material needed for each shipment, warehouses can reduce overpacking, reuse packaging materials, and minimize waste generation.

Waste Stream Analysis: Predictive models can also be used to track the generation of different types of waste within the warehouse, such as cardboard, plastic, or electronic waste. By identifying waste trends, warehouses can predict when waste levels will peak and implement targeted strategies to reduce or recycle these materials. This not only minimizes landfill waste but also reduces disposal costs.

Inventory Turnover and Spoilage Reduction: In warehouses that handle perishable goods, predictive analytics helps optimize inventory turnover and reduce spoilage. By analyzing historical sales data, demand fluctuations, and product shelf life, predictive models can forecast when stock is likely to expire or become obsolete. This allows warehouses to adjust stock levels accordingly and implement strategies such as early discounting or donating products to reduce waste and avoid product loss.

Optimizing Inventory Levels to Avoid Overstocking

Inventory management is critical to sustainable warehousing. Overstocking leads to increased storage costs, unnecessary resource consumption, and higher waste levels, particularly for products that may become obsolete or expire. Big data and analytics play an essential role in ensuring that inventory levels are optimized, minimizing waste while meeting customer demand.

1. Demand Forecasting with Big Data

Predicting customer demand accurately is crucial to avoiding overstocking and understocking, both of which can have negative environmental impacts. By leveraging big data and advanced analytics, warehouses can forecast demand more accurately and optimize their inventory levels to meet customer needs without excessive overstock.

Historical Sales Data: One of the primary sources of demand forecasting is historical sales data. By analyzing past sales patterns, including seasonal trends, product popularity, and regional variations, warehouses can make more accurate predictions about future demand. Predictive analytics tools use this data to identify trends and adjust inventory levels accordingly, ensuring that warehouses only stock what is necessary to fulfill customer orders.

External Data Integration: Beyond historical sales data, external factors such as weather conditions, market trends, and economic indicators can also influence demand. By integrating external data into the forecasting models, warehouses can refine their predictions and adjust inventory levels in real-time to reflect changes in demand. For instance, a sudden cold snap may drive up demand for winter apparel, prompting warehouses to increase inventory levels in anticipation of customer orders.

Customer Behavior and Social Media Analysis: Advanced analytics can also analyze customer behavior and social media trends to predict shifts in demand. For example, a product that becomes popular due to a social media campaign or influencer endorsement may experience a surge in demand. By analyzing these factors in real-time, warehouses can adjust their inventory strategies to respond quickly to changes in customer behavior, avoiding overstocking or stockouts.

2. Just-In-Time Inventory and Lean Practices

One of the most effective ways to avoid overstocking is by implementing just-in-time (JIT) inventory management and lean warehousing practices. JIT inventory involves receiving goods only as they are needed in the production process or to fulfill customer orders, which helps reduce inventory levels and minimize waste.

Data-Driven JIT: Big data and predictive analytics make JIT inventory management more effective by providing real-time insights into inventory levels, order trends, and supplier lead times. This enables warehouses to place orders with suppliers based on accurate demand forecasts, reducing the need to keep large quantities of stock on hand. By using predictive models, warehouses can also anticipate fluctuations in demand, ensuring they have enough stock to meet customer needs without excess inventory.

Optimizing Replenishment Cycles: Predictive analytics can also optimize replenishment cycles by forecasting when stocks will run low based on current sales data. This ensures that inventory is replenished at the right time to prevent stockouts while avoiding overstocking. By fine-tuning replenishment schedules, warehouses can reduce the amount of unsold stock that sits idle in the warehouse, minimizing waste and maximizing efficiency.

Inventory Turnover Rate Optimization: The inventory turnover rate is a critical metric for measuring how quickly inventory is sold and replaced. Big data and analytics tools enable warehouses to track this rate more accurately and adjust stock levels to improve turnover. By optimizing inventory turnover, warehouses can minimize the need for excessive stock storage and reduce waste caused by obsolete or unsold products.

3. Real-Time Tracking and Automated Inventory Management

Real-time tracking of inventory levels, combined with automated inventory management systems, further enhances the ability of warehouses to avoid overstocking and optimize storage. IoT-enabled sensors and RFID technology can track products as they move through the warehouse, providing real-time data on stock levels and product locations.

Automated Reordering Systems: With the integration of real-time tracking data and analytics, automated reordering systems can ensure that inventory levels remain balanced. These systems can automatically place orders with suppliers when stock reaches predefined thresholds, preventing both overstocking and stockouts. Automated systems use predictive analytics to adjust reorder points based on demand trends and historical data, optimizing inventory levels with minimal manual intervention.

Smart Shelving and Slotting: Big data analytics can optimize shelving and slotting strategies, ensuring that high-demand products are stored in easily accessible locations while reducing unnecessary storage of low-demand items. This minimizes the need for excessive stock and improves warehouse space utilization.

Big data and analytics have become indispensable tools in creating sustainable warehouses. Predictive analytics for energy and waste reduction allows warehouses to forecast energy consumption, optimize resource use, and reduce waste generation. At the same time, optimizing inventory levels through data-driven demand forecasting, JIT inventory, and automated systems helps prevent overstocking, reducing waste and storage costs. By integrating these technologies into their operations, warehouses can significantly improve their sustainability while maintaining operational efficiency and reducing their environmental footprint.

Smart Warehouse Management Systems (WMS)

In recent years, warehouse management systems (WMS) have evolved significantly, shifting from traditional, manual inventory tracking to more advanced, automated systems that improve both operational efficiency and sustainability. Smart WMS, designed with cutting-edge technology and sustainability in mind, offers a range of features that help warehouses optimize their operations while reducing their environmental impact. As warehouses increasingly prioritize eco-friendly practices, the integration of these smart systems plays a critical role in promoting green warehousing and aligning business operations with sustainable development goals.

This chapter will explore the features of eco-friendly warehouse management systems (WMS) and provide examples of sustainable WMS implementations across various industries.

Features of Eco-Friendly WMS

Eco-friendly WMS are designed to enhance the environmental performance of warehouse operations while improving overall efficiency and reducing operational costs. These systems incorporate various features that promote sustainability in warehouse activities, such as energy management, resource optimization, waste reduction, and improved supply chain visibility. Some key features of an eco-friendly WMS include:

1. Real-Time Inventory Tracking and Optimization

One of the most important features of a smart WMS is the ability to track inventory in real time. By using technologies like RFID (Radio Frequency Identification) and barcode scanning, warehouses can monitor the movement of products and materials with accuracy. This real-time tracking minimizes the need for excess inventory and reduces the chances of overstocking, which in turn helps prevent waste and the unnecessary consumption of resources.

Optimized Stock Levels: Through integration with predictive analytics, smart WMS systems can help forecast demand accurately. This allows warehouses to adjust stock levels to meet actual demand, avoiding both stockouts and excess stock that requires additional storage space and energy consumption.

Reduced Waste: Efficient inventory tracking ensures that products, especially perishable goods, are sold or used before their expiration date, minimizing waste. This also prevents the need to dispose of outdated or unsold items that might have otherwise ended up in landfills.

2. Energy Consumption Management

Eco-friendly WMS integrates with energy management systems to optimize energy usage throughout the warehouse. From reducing lighting needs to managing HVAC systems, these systems help minimize energy waste.

Smart Lighting and HVAC Systems: By incorporating IoT sensors and advanced algorithms, WMS can control lighting and heating/cooling systems based on real-time activity and occupancy in different areas of the warehouse. For example, lights can automatically adjust depending on foot traffic, and HVAC systems can be optimized based on the warehouse's specific climate needs. This reduces overall energy consumption by eliminating unnecessary energy use.

Energy Data Monitoring: With data analytics, a smart WMS can track energy consumption patterns, enabling managers to identify areas of inefficiency and implement changes to reduce energy consumption. This may include shifting energy-intensive tasks to off-peak hours or optimizing equipment performance to ensure energy use is at its most efficient.

3. Automated Material Handling and Resource Allocation

Material handling and resource allocation are critical components of warehouse operations. A smart WMS can automate these processes, reducing the need for manual labor and energy-intensive equipment. Automation systems such as robotic picking and automated guided vehicles (AGVs) work in tandem with the WMS to optimize workflows and reduce energy consumption.

Efficient Equipment Utilization: With a smart WMS, warehouses can optimize the usage of automated material handling equipment by tracking their performance and usage patterns. This ensures that equipment is only used when necessary, reducing idle time and energy waste.

Reduced Carbon Footprint: Automation also reduces the need for excessive transportation within the warehouse, cutting down on fuel consumption and emissions from vehicles and forklifts. This contributes to a greener, more efficient operation overall.

4. Waste Reduction and Recycling Integration

Waste reduction is a major component of sustainable warehousing, and an eco-friendly WMS plays a key role in minimizing waste. These systems can be integrated with waste management programs to track and manage waste production, ensuring that materials are reused, recycled, or disposed of in an environmentally friendly manner.

Waste Stream Monitoring: A smart WMS can categorize and track waste materials such as cardboard, plastic, and other packaging materials. By analyzing waste data, the system can help identify opportunities for recycling, reducing the need for new materials and minimizing landfill waste.

Packaging Optimization: The WMS can optimize packaging processes by ensuring that the right amount of packaging is used, reducing excess materials. This reduces waste from packaging materials while still ensuring products are protected during transit.

5. Optimizing Transportation and Distribution

A smart WMS is also capable of optimizing transportation routes and delivery schedules, reducing unnecessary fuel consumption and carbon emissions in the supply chain.

Route Optimization: By integrating with transportation management systems (TMS), a WMS can suggest the most fuel-efficient routes for delivery trucks. This minimizes the carbon footprint of transporting goods, ensuring that trucks take the shortest and least congested routes while reducing fuel consumption.

Consolidation of Shipments: The WMS can help optimize order fulfillment and consolidate shipments, reducing the number of deliveries required. By grouping orders based on proximity or delivery time windows, warehouses can reduce the number of trips and overall fuel usage, further contributing to sustainability.

Examples of Sustainable WMS Implementations

Several companies across industries have successfully implemented smart and eco-friendly WMS to improve their sustainability efforts. Here are a few notable examples:

1. Amazon's Use of Robotics and Automation

Amazon is a leader in integrating technology into its warehousing operations, and its use of smart WMS in conjunction with robotics and automation is a prime example of how WMS can contribute to sustainability. Amazon's fulfillment centers utilize robots and automated systems for material handling, which reduces the need for energy-intensive human labor and increases efficiency. The company's WMS integrates real-time tracking, energy management, and predictive analytics, ensuring that inventory levels are optimized, energy use is minimized, and waste is reduced. Additionally, Amazon's use of electric-powered robots in their warehouses has further minimized the carbon footprint of their operations.

2. Walmart's Sustainability Initiatives

Walmart has integrated eco-friendly WMS into its global supply chain to streamline operations while minimizing environmental impact. Their smart WMS utilizes real-time inventory tracking, energy management, and waste reduction techniques to support their sustainability goals. For example, Walmart has implemented automated systems that allow for more efficient stock replenishment, ensuring that inventory levels align with customer demand, thus reducing overstock and waste. Additionally, the company has committed to using renewable energy sources in its distribution centers and has been focusing on reducing packaging waste through the implementation of optimized packaging solutions within their WMS.

3. IKEA's Green Warehousing

IKEA has committed to sustainability across its operations, including warehousing. Its smart WMS integrates energy-efficient systems, such as smart lighting and HVAC controls, to reduce energy consumption. The system is also designed to optimize inventory levels and minimize waste. For example, by using data from their WMS, IKEA has been able to reduce the overstock of certain furniture items, thereby lowering waste and unnecessary energy usage in storing and handling unsold products. The company has also integrated its WMS with its recycling program, ensuring that packaging materials are recycled and reused efficiently.

4. Unilever's Eco-Friendly Distribution Centers

Unilever is another company that has made significant strides in incorporating sustainability into its warehousing operations. The company's eco-friendly WMS plays a crucial role in managing energy consumption, waste reduction, and transportation optimization. By using IoT sensors and real-time data, Unilever has optimized inventory and storage, reducing unnecessary energy use and ensuring that their warehouses run at maximum efficiency. The company has also integrated its WMS with its sustainability programs, ensuring that waste from production and packaging is recycled and managed effectively.

Smart WMS are essential tools for warehouses looking to enhance their sustainability practices. Through energy management, waste reduction, real-time inventory tracking, and resource optimization, eco-friendly WMS contribute to creating more sustainable operations. By implementing automation, optimizing transportation, and integrating with renewable energy sources, businesses can drastically reduce their environmental footprint while improving operational efficiency. As demonstrated by industry leaders like Amazon, Walmart, IKEA, and Unilever, the integration of sustainable WMS into warehouse operations is not only possible but essential for future growth and environmental responsibility.

PartV:Sustainable Transportation and Logistics

Eco-Friendly Transportation Strategies

In the quest for sustainability, the logistics and transportation sector plays a crucial role in reducing the carbon footprint of supply chains. Warehouses, distribution centers, and other logistics operations are inherently connected to transportation systems, and as such, transitioning to eco-friendly transportation strategies is an essential aspect of creating a sustainable warehouse environment. Implementing green transportation practices not only helps reduce greenhouse gas emissions but also leads to cost savings, improved efficiency, and enhanced brand reputation.

This chapter explores eco-friendly transportation strategies that warehouses and logistics companies can adopt, with a focus on the shift to electric and hybrid vehicles and optimizing routes and load planning.

1. Shift to Electric and Hybrid Vehicles

One of the most impactful ways to reduce the environmental footprint of transportation is by shifting from traditional internal combustion engine (ICE) vehicles to electric (EV) and hybrid vehicles. These vehicles produce far fewer emissions, lower noise pollution, and, in the case of fully electric vehicles, eliminate tailpipe emissions altogether. Transitioning to electric and hybrid vehicles offers a range of environmental and operational benefits for logistics and warehousing companies.

Electric Vehicles (EVs)

Electric vehicles are powered entirely by electricity, typically drawn from renewable energy sources, and thus do not rely on fossil fuels. For warehouses and logistics operations, EVs offer several key advantages:

Reduction in Greenhouse Gas Emissions: Unlike conventional vehicles that run on gasoline or diesel, EVs produce no tailpipe emissions, significantly lowering the greenhouse gases released into the atmosphere. When charged using renewable energy sources such as solar or wind power, the carbon footprint of these vehicles can be reduced to near zero, making them a critical part of a sustainable transportation strategy.

Lower Operating Costs: While the initial purchase cost of electric vehicles may be higher than traditional vehicles, they offer long-term cost savings. EVs have lower maintenance costs, as they have fewer moving parts compared to ICE vehicles. Additionally, the cost of electricity is often lower than gasoline or diesel fuel, further reducing operational costs.

Improved Air Quality: EVs contribute to better air quality in urban and industrial areas, where delivery trucks and transportation vehicles are often concentrated. By reducing the amount of particulate matter and nitrogen oxide emissions from traditional diesel engines, electric trucks help reduce the negative health impacts associated with poor air quality, particularly in densely populated areas.

Hybrid Vehicles

Hybrid vehicles combine an internal combustion engine with an electric motor, allowing them to operate on both electricity and traditional fuel. This dual power source helps optimize fuel consumption, reduce emissions, and improve fuel efficiency.

Fuel Efficiency: Hybrid vehicles are particularly useful for short-haul delivery routes, where they can operate on electric power in urban environments and switch to fuel power for longer trips. By optimizing fuel consumption, hybrid vehicles reduce overall carbon emissions and operational costs.

Range and Flexibility: Unlike fully electric vehicles, hybrids have a greater range, making them suitable for longer trips that may exceed the battery life of EVs. They provide flexibility for operations that require a combination of both long-distance and city-based deliveries.

Cost-effective Solution: For companies that may not yet have the infrastructure to support a full electric fleet, hybrid vehicles provide a more affordable and practical transition. They offer the environmental benefits of electric vehicles while still retaining the reliability and range of traditional vehicles.

2. Optimizing Routes and Load Planning

In addition to adopting electric and hybrid vehicles, optimizing transportation routes and load planning is another key strategy for reducing the environmental impact of logistics operations. By improving the efficiency of transportation routes and maximizing the capacity of delivery vehicles, companies can reduce the total distance traveled, fuel consumption, and emissions associated with their transportation activities.

Route Optimization

Route optimization involves planning the most efficient routes for transportation vehicles to follow, taking into account factors such as distance, traffic patterns, road conditions, and delivery time windows. By using sophisticated algorithms and real-time data, logistics companies can reduce unnecessary mileage, fuel consumption, and carbon emissions.

Traffic and Weather Data: Advanced route optimization software uses real-time data on traffic conditions, weather, and road closures to dynamically adjust routes, ensuring that drivers avoid congested areas and delays. This not only improves fuel efficiency but also reduces the time spent on the road, leading to lower emissions.

Geofencing: Geofencing technology allows logistics companies to create virtual boundaries around specific areas, such as low-emission zones or urban centers. Vehicles can be routed to avoid these zones, reducing emissions in sensitive areas and complying with local environmental regulations.

Eco-driving Features: Many route optimization systems now include eco-driving features that provide real-time feedback to drivers, helping them optimize their driving habits. For example, systems can suggest lower-speed routes, smoother driving styles, or adjustments to acceleration patterns to reduce fuel consumption and emissions.

Load Planning

Load planning is the process of determining how to best distribute products within a vehicle, optimizing available space and ensuring that deliveries are as efficient as possible. By maximizing load capacity, companies can reduce the number of trips required to transport goods, resulting in less fuel consumption and fewer emissions.

Maximizing Vehicle Utilization: By carefully planning how goods are loaded into transportation vehicles, logistics companies can ensure that trucks are fully loaded, reducing the need for additional trips. This helps decrease fuel consumption and the associated carbon footprint.

Multi-stop Deliveries: Load planning can also involve consolidating multiple deliveries into a single trip. By grouping deliveries that are geographically close together, logistics companies can minimize the number of trips required to deliver products, improving efficiency and reducing emissions.

Freight Consolidation: In some cases, logistics companies can work with other businesses to consolidate freight. Shared delivery arrangements enable multiple companies to share space on a single vehicle, reducing the overall number of vehicles on the road and contributing to lower emissions and fuel consumption.

3. Environmental Impact of Eco-Friendly Transportation

The adoption of electric and hybrid vehicles, along with optimized routes and load planning, can have a profound impact on the environment. These eco-friendly transportation strategies reduce the overall carbon footprint of the logistics industry, which is one of the largest contributors to global greenhouse gas emissions.

Reduction in Carbon Emissions: By shifting to electric and hybrid vehicles and optimizing routes, logistics companies can significantly lower their carbon emissions. This is particularly important in reducing the overall greenhouse gas emissions from the transportation sector, which contributes heavily to global warming and climate change.

Air Quality Improvements: The reduction in vehicle emissions not only helps lower greenhouse gases but also improves air quality, particularly in urban areas where pollution levels are often high. By reducing the number of diesel-powered trucks on the road, logistics companies can help reduce smog and other harmful pollutants that affect public health.

Lower Noise Pollution: Electric vehicles, in particular, operate with minimal noise, which reduces noise pollution in densely populated areas. This is a significant benefit in urban logistics, where the constant noise of trucks can have detrimental effects on residents' well-being.

Decreased Resource Consumption: By optimizing load planning and reducing unnecessary trips, logistics companies can also decrease the overall consumption of fuel and other resources, further contributing to a more sustainable supply chain.

Eco-friendly transportation strategies, including the shift to electric and hybrid vehicles and the optimization of routes and load planning, are critical components of sustainable logistics operations. These strategies not only help reduce carbon emissions and lower operational costs but also contribute to a greener, more efficient supply chain. As the logistics industry continues to evolve, embracing these eco-friendly practices will be key to reducing the environmental impact of transportation while ensuring the continued success and competitiveness of businesses in a rapidly changing world.

Part V: Sustainable Transportation and Logistics

Carbon Footprint Reduction in Warehousing

As industries and organizations worldwide strive to become more sustainable, one of the critical goals is reducing the carbon footprint associated with their operations. In warehousing, the carbon footprint primarily results from energy consumption, transportation, waste, and the materials used in construction and day-to-day operations. With the increasing demand for sustainable business practices, the reduction of carbon emissions in warehouses is gaining importance not only for environmental reasons but also due to growing regulatory pressures, cost efficiency, and consumer preference for green businesses.

This chapter explores the tools and strategies available for measuring and reducing the carbon footprint in warehouses. It will also discuss carbon offset programs as an important part of the solution, especially when it comes to mitigating unavoidable emissions.

1. Tools for Measuring and Reducing Carbon Emissions

A key step in managing and reducing carbon emissions is understanding the scale of the problem. To achieve effective carbon footprint reduction, warehouses must first measure the amount of carbon they emit. Several tools and methods are available for this purpose, each offering insights into various aspects of warehouse operations.

Carbon Footprint Measurement Tools

Several tools are available to warehouses to measure their carbon footprint. These tools can calculate emissions from different sources such as energy use, transportation, waste, and more.

Carbon Footprint Calculators: There are several online calculators and software solutions designed to estimate the carbon emissions of an organization based on the energy consumption, fleet usage, waste production, and other relevant metrics. Examples include tools offered by carbon management companies like the Carbon Trust and Greenhouse Gas Protocol. These calculators allow businesses to input data about electricity consumption, fuel usage, waste generation, and other key factors to calculate their total carbon emissions.

Life Cycle Assessment (LCA): Life Cycle Assessment is a comprehensive method for evaluating the environmental impact of a product or process from cradle to grave, including all phases such as manufacturing, transportation, use, and disposal. LCAs can be used in warehousing to assess the carbon impact of equipment, building materials, and overall operations. Through an LCA, warehouses can identify opportunities for improvement across all stages of the supply chain and implement reductions in their carbon footprint.

Energy Monitoring Systems: By using energy management systems (EMS) and building management systems (BMS), warehouses can monitor their energy usage in real time. These systems collect data on electricity consumption, heating, and cooling, which allows warehouses to detect inefficiencies and identify areas where energy usage can be reduced. Smart meters and IoT sensors can provide granular data, and integrating this information into a warehouse's energy strategy allows for targeted emissions reductions.

Transportation Emission Estimators: Since transportation is a significant contributor to warehouse carbon footprints, estimating emissions from logistics operations is crucial. There are specialized tools that can estimate emissions from vehicle fleets. These tools take into account factors like fuel consumption, the type of vehicle, the distance traveled, and the cargo load to provide an accurate assessment of transportation-related emissions.

Strategies for Reducing Carbon Emissions

Once carbon emissions have been measured, warehouses can use several strategies to reduce their carbon footprint. Here are some effective methods:

Energy Efficiency Improvements: One of the most significant sources of emissions in warehouses is energy consumption. Implementing energy-efficient lighting (such as LEDs), upgrading HVAC systems, and enhancing insulation are all effective strategies to reduce energy usage. Additionally, adopting energy-efficient equipment like forklifts and automated systems can also cut energy consumption in daily operations.

Use of Renewable Energy: Switching to renewable energy sources such as solar, wind, or geothermal power can significantly reduce a warehouse's carbon footprint. Installing solar panels on the roof of a warehouse or contracting with a green energy provider can help decrease reliance on fossil fuels and lower overall emissions. Some warehouses may even generate surplus energy, which can be stored or sold back to the grid.

Optimized Warehouse Layout and Operations: Efficient space utilization and operational design can help reduce energy consumption. For example, warehouses can optimize racking systems to ensure better airflow and reduce the need for artificial cooling. Implementing energy-efficient material handling systems, like automated conveyor belts or robotic systems, can reduce energy usage while improving operational efficiency.

Green Building Standards: Implementing sustainable building materials, energy-efficient insulation, high-performance windows, and green construction methods can drastically reduce a warehouse's energy consumption and carbon emissions. Certifications like LEED (Leadership in Energy and Environmental Design) or ISO 14001 are benchmarks that ensure a building is constructed with sustainability in mind, thus reducing the long-term carbon footprint.

Efficient Transportation and Delivery Planning: Efficient logistics is a significant part of carbon footprint reduction. Optimizing delivery routes, switching to electric or hybrid trucks, consolidating shipments, and reducing empty miles can all help reduce the carbon emissions associated with transportation. Analyzing transportation data with route optimization software can reduce fuel consumption and emissions.

2. Carbon Offset Programs

While reducing carbon emissions through operational improvements is the first and most critical step, some emissions may still be unavoidable. In such cases, carbon offset programs provide a way for warehouses to balance out the emissions they generate by investing in projects that reduce or capture an equivalent amount of carbon elsewhere.

How Carbon Offsetting Works

Carbon offset programs allow businesses to compensate for their carbon emissions by funding projects that either reduce or absorb greenhouse gases. These projects can range from renewable energy initiatives, reforestation efforts, and methane capture projects, to technologies that reduce emissions in other industries.

Reforestation and Afforestation: Trees naturally absorb carbon dioxide as part of their growth process. Carbon offset programs often invest in tree planting and forest conservation efforts, which help absorb the carbon dioxide produced by businesses. Projects that restore or create forests contribute directly to reducing atmospheric carbon levels.

Renewable Energy Projects: Offsetting carbon emissions by investing in renewable energy projects is another way businesses can compensate for their emissions. This might include funding wind farms, solar energy projects, or other clean energy infrastructure projects that displace the need for fossil fuel-based electricity generation.

Methane Capture: Methane is a potent greenhouse gas that is often released from landfills and agricultural operations. Carbon offset programs can involve projects that capture methane emissions and convert them into usable energy, reducing their environmental impact.

Energy Efficiency Projects: Offsetting can also involve supporting projects that improve energy efficiency in industries or communities. For example, funding energy-efficient cookstoves for developing countries or upgrading buildings to be more energy-efficient can directly reduce carbon emissions on a large scale.

Selecting the Right Carbon Offset Program

When selecting a carbon offset program, warehouses should ensure that the projects they fund are verifiable, transparent, and certified by credible standards. Some of the most well-known standards for carbon offset verification include:

Verified Carbon Standard (VCS): This is one of the most widely recognized certification standards for carbon offset projects. VCS ensures that projects meet rigorous requirements and result in real, measurable, and permanent carbon reductions.

Gold Standard: Created by the WWF and other environmental NGOs, the Gold Standard ensures that offset projects deliver high environmental and social benefits. Gold Standard projects focus on renewable energy, sustainable development, and community well-being.

Climate, Community & Biodiversity Standards (CCBS): These standards assess the impacts of carbon offset projects on the environment, biodiversity, and communities, ensuring that they deliver sustainable development alongside carbon reduction.

Integrating Carbon Offsetting into a Warehouse's Sustainability Strategy

Incorporating carbon offsetting into a warehouse's sustainability strategy can be a key component of its overall emissions reduction efforts. While it should not be seen as a replacement for direct emissions reductions, offsetting can serve as an effective tool for balancing out emissions that cannot be eliminated. By purchasing offsets that support credible and impactful projects, warehouses can contribute to global sustainability efforts and bolster their environmental credentials.

Reducing the carbon footprint in warehouses is an essential aspect of creating a sustainable supply chain and mitigating the effects of climate change. Through the use of carbon footprint measurement tools, warehouses can track their emissions and identify areas for improvement. By implementing energy efficiency measures, transitioning to renewable energy, optimizing operations, and adopting green building standards, warehouses can significantly reduce their emissions. For those emissions that remain unavoidable, carbon offset programs provide a valuable way to mitigate environmental impact, allowing warehouses to contribute to global sustainability efforts. By combining direct reduction efforts with carbon offsetting, warehouses can take a proactive approach to managing their environmental footprint while maintaining operational efficiency and cost-effectiveness.

Part VI: Workforce and Community Engagement

Building a Culture of Sustainability

In the transition towards sustainable warehousing practices, one of the most vital elements of success is building a culture of sustainability. This requires fostering a mindset within the workforce that prioritizes environmental responsibility, economic efficiency, and social well-being. In a warehouse setting, where daily operations can have a significant environmental impact, cultivating a culture of sustainability is essential for not only achieving environmental goals but also for engaging employees, enhancing productivity, and ensuring long-term success.

The culture of sustainability in warehousing involves much more than just implementing green practices; it requires the active participation and buy-in of every employee, from leadership to front-line workers. In this chapter, we will explore the strategies for building a culture of sustainability, focusing on training employees on green practices and encouraging a sustainability mindset across all levels of the organization.

1. Training Employees on Green Practices

One of the first steps in building a sustainability-driven culture is to provide employees with the knowledge and skills necessary to implement green practices effectively. Training is essential to ensure that all staff members understand the importance of sustainability, the company's environmental goals, and how their roles contribute to achieving those goals.

Green Practices Training Programs

For a warehouse to successfully incorporate sustainability into its operations, it is crucial to develop and deliver comprehensive training programs that address various aspects of green practices. These programs should focus on practical, actionable steps employees can take in their daily routines.

Energy Efficiency Training: One of the most straightforward ways to reduce a warehouse's carbon footprint is by promoting energy efficiency. Employees should be trained on energy-saving techniques such as turning off lights and equipment when not in use, optimizing heating and cooling systems, and utilizing energy-efficient equipment. Understanding the importance of energy efficiency and how their actions can make a difference is critical for staff to contribute effectively to the warehouse's sustainability goals.

Waste Reduction and Recycling: Waste management plays a significant role in reducing environmental impacts in a warehouse. Training employees on proper recycling techniques, separating materials, and minimizing waste from packaging and operations can lead to significant reductions in landfill waste. Providing knowledge on composting and waste reduction strategies helps employees feel empowered to contribute to a circular economy within the warehouse environment.

Sustainable Material Handling: Employees should also be trained on using eco-friendly packaging materials and sustainable handling practices. This includes understanding the types of materials that can be recycled or reused, as well as minimizing the waste generated during the process. For instance, using reusable containers, eliminating single-use plastics, and applying just-in-time (JIT) inventory systems can reduce waste and improve operational efficiency.

Health and Safety in Green Practices: Sustainable practices in warehousing should not only focus on environmental benefits but also on improving the safety and well-being of employees. Training should emphasize the safety protocols associated with handling green materials, such as those used in energy-efficient equipment or in waste management processes. Proper training ensures that employees know how to handle sustainable technologies, such as solar panels, wind turbines, and electric vehicles, without compromising their safety.

Ongoing Education and Engagement

Sustainability training should not be a one-time event. To foster a culture of sustainability, it is crucial that companies provide ongoing education, reinforcement, and updates on green initiatives.

Sustainability Workshops and Seminars: Regular workshops and seminars focusing on new trends in sustainability and best practices in green warehousing can keep employees informed and engaged. These forums can also be used to introduce new technologies and strategies for reducing carbon footprints and other environmental impacts. By creating a space where employees can learn from experts, discuss their challenges, and exchange ideas, companies can keep sustainability at the forefront of the warehouse culture.

Sustainability Incentive Programs: To encourage employees to adopt green practices, warehouses can create incentive programs that reward individuals or teams for implementing energy-saving measures, reducing waste, or achieving sustainability targets. These rewards can range from monetary bonuses to recognition in company newsletters, fostering a sense of accomplishment and motivation among staff.

Interactive Learning Tools: Integrating gamified learning platforms or sustainability challenges into the training process can make the educational experience more engaging and rewarding for employees. Interactive tools such as quizzes, virtual simulations, or competitions can increase employee participation and deepen their understanding of green practices.

2. Encouraging a Sustainability Mindset

Building a culture of sustainability is not just about training employees on green practices; it is about shifting their mindset so that sustainability becomes an intrinsic part of their daily operations and decision-making processes. Encouraging a sustainability mindset goes beyond compliance with green initiatives—it is about instilling an ethos that considers the long-term impact of their actions on the environment, the community, and the business itself.

Leadership Commitment and Role Modeling

A sustainable culture must start at the top. Leaders in the organization play a critical role in fostering a sustainability mindset by setting clear examples, communicating the importance of sustainability, and providing the necessary resources and support for employees to adopt green practices.

Leading by Example: When senior leaders and managers actively participate in green initiatives, it sends a powerful message to employees. Whether it's reducing paper usage, supporting energy-saving programs, or engaging in carbon offset projects, leadership's visible commitment to sustainability demonstrates that it is a priority for the entire organization. Leaders should also publicly acknowledge and celebrate sustainability milestones, such as reducing energy consumption by a certain percentage or achieving zero waste to landfill.

Clear Vision and Communication: Establishing and communicating a clear vision of sustainability is essential for engaging employees. This vision should align with the company's overall mission and values and provide a roadmap for how sustainability fits into the warehouse's operations. Regularly communicating the company's sustainability goals and progress through meetings, newsletters, or digital platforms ensures that everyone stays aligned and motivated.

Creating a Collaborative Sustainability Culture

Sustainability is not a siloed responsibility; it must involve collaboration across all departments and levels of the organization. Encouraging open communication, teamwork, and cross-departmental collaboration on sustainability initiatives can help foster a collective responsibility for environmental stewardship.

Team-Based Sustainability Goals: Assigning sustainability-related objectives to teams or departments, such as reducing energy consumption in a specific section of the warehouse or increasing recycling rates in the packaging area, encourages collective ownership of sustainability goals. These goals should be measurable and tied to key performance indicators (KPIs) to track progress and ensure accountability.

Employee Feedback and Ideas: Employees often have valuable insights into how sustainability can be improved in their specific work areas. By encouraging feedback, suggestions, and innovation from employees, warehouses can tap into creative solutions that may not have been considered at the management level. This could be through suggestion boxes, employee surveys, or sustainability committees where staff can collaborate on new ideas and innovations.

Sustainability as a Shared Value: Creating a sense of shared responsibility for sustainability makes employees feel that they are part of something larger than themselves. In this context, sustainability becomes a core value of the company that influences decision-making at every level. When employees see how their individual actions contribute to broader sustainability goals, they are more likely to adopt green practices and share the company's commitment to the environment.

Recognizing and Celebrating Sustainability Achievements

Recognition is an essential tool for reinforcing a culture of sustainability. Acknowledging and celebrating the contributions of employees and teams not only reinforces positive behaviors but also motivates others to engage with sustainability initiatives. This recognition can take many forms:

Employee of the Month Programs: Recognizing employees who have gone above and beyond in implementing sustainable practices, whether by suggesting energy-saving ideas or leading a successful recycling initiative, encourages others to follow suit.

Sustainability Awards and Certifications: Offering awards for sustainability achievements, such as "Green Warehouse of the Year," can motivate employees to strive for excellence in implementing sustainability initiatives. These awards could be presented at company-wide events to celebrate and publicly acknowledge the efforts of individuals and teams.

Celebrating Milestones: When the warehouse achieves a significant sustainability milestone—whether it's a reduction in energy consumption, waste diversion, or carbon emissions—celebrate these accomplishments with the entire team. Milestones provide tangible proof that sustainability efforts are making a difference, and this recognition fosters a sense of pride and ownership among employees.

Building a culture of sustainability in warehousing is not just about implementing eco-friendly practices—it is about integrating sustainability into the very fabric of the organization. Training employees on green practices, encouraging a sustainability mindset, and providing leadership and recognition are all critical components of this transformation. When employees feel informed, empowered, and motivated to contribute to sustainability efforts, they become active participants in the organization's environmental goals. This cultural shift towards sustainability not only enhances the environmental impact of warehousing operations but also improves employee satisfaction, loyalty, and productivity, making it a win-win for businesses committed to a greener future.

Community and Stakeholder Engagement

In the pursuit of sustainability, the role of community and stakeholder engagement cannot be overstated. For warehouses and distribution centers, creating a positive relationship with local communities and maintaining transparency with stakeholders is integral to the success of sustainability efforts. Effective community and stakeholder engagement goes beyond compliance and greenwashing; it involves genuine collaboration and long-term commitment to social, environmental, and economic responsibility.

This chapter delves into the ways warehouses can engage with local communities and stakeholders, focusing on the importance of partnering with local communities and maintaining transparency through sustainability reporting.

1. Partnering with Local Communities

Sustainable warehousing practices are not just confined to the four walls of the warehouse itself. The impact of warehouse operations extends to the surrounding community in numerous ways, from environmental effects such as air and water quality to social effects, such as job creation and community well-being. Warehouses can forge mutually beneficial relationships with local communities, ensuring that their sustainability efforts have a broader, positive impact.

Supporting Local Economies

One of the most direct ways warehouses can engage with their local communities is by supporting local economies. Sourcing materials locally, for example, not only reduces the carbon footprint associated with transportation but also contributes to the economic growth of the region. This local sourcing can also build stronger ties with suppliers, help boost employment opportunities, and support local businesses, all of which contribute to the community's resilience and sustainability.

Local Supplier Engagement: By purchasing materials and services from local suppliers, warehouses can reduce transportation emissions while stimulating local businesses. These suppliers may include packaging providers, maintenance services, or even energy solutions. The more a warehouse works with local vendors, the more it strengthens the economic fabric of the community. Furthermore, local sourcing helps minimize supply chain disruptions by reducing reliance on international suppliers and global shipping routes.

Job Creation and Training: Warehouses can engage with local communities by creating job opportunities, especially in areas where employment may be scarce. By hiring locally and offering job training programs, warehouses can help develop the skills of the local workforce. This can lead to increased economic opportunities and improved livelihoods for community members. Additionally, training programs in sustainable practices, such as energy efficiency or waste management, can upskill workers and prepare them for the future of green industries.

Collaborating on Local Environmental Initiatives: Warehouses can also partner with local organizations and environmental groups to address shared environmental concerns. For instance, they might support local clean-up projects, plant trees, or collaborate on community education campaigns around sustainability. These partnerships can help warehouses align their environmental goals with those of the broader community, making sustainability a shared endeavor.

Community Well-Being and Engagement

Sustainable warehouses should aim to enhance the quality of life in their surrounding communities. This can be achieved by considering the broader social impacts of warehouse operations, such as the effects on air and water quality, traffic, and noise pollution.

Minimizing Environmental Footprint: One of the core ways warehouses can partner with communities is by reducing their environmental footprint. This includes minimizing air and water pollution and controlling noise levels. Warehouses located near residential or recreational areas can implement measures to reduce emissions from machinery and vehicles, as well as control noise pollution through soundproofing and limiting operating hours during the night.

Providing Community Benefits: Beyond minimizing negative impacts, warehouses can give back to their local communities through social investments, such as donations to local charities, sponsoring events, or supporting community development programs. For example, a warehouse could sponsor local schools' environmental education programs or fund green infrastructure projects like parks or bicycle paths, aligning the warehouse's sustainability efforts with the well-being of the local population.

Building Trust and Collaboration: By actively participating in community activities and being transparent about their sustainability initiatives, warehouses can build trust with the public. This openness fosters goodwill and shows that the business is genuinely interested in the community's welfare, not just its own success. Regular community meetings, open houses, and participation in local environmental initiatives are all excellent ways to engage directly with residents and local organizations.

2. Transparency and Reporting in Sustainability

Transparency is a critical element in any successful sustainability strategy. Stakeholders—whether they are investors, customers, employees, or members of the local community—are increasingly demanding visibility into the environmental and social practices of companies, including warehouses. Transparent sustainability reporting not only builds credibility but also reinforces the warehouse's commitment to ethical practices and continuous improvement.

Sustainability Reporting Standards

Sustainability reporting involves the disclosure of a company's environmental, social, and economic performance. For warehouses, this can include reporting on energy consumption, waste generation, water usage, greenhouse gas emissions, employee welfare, and community engagement. To ensure the reports are credible and meaningful, they must align with established standards and frameworks.

Global Reporting Initiative (GRI): One of the most widely used sustainability reporting frameworks is the Global Reporting Initiative (GRI). The GRI provides standardized guidelines for companies to measure and report their sustainability impacts. By adopting the GRI standards, warehouses can ensure that their sustainability reports are comprehensive, transparent, and comparable to industry benchmarks.

Carbon Disclosure Project (CDP): Another well-known reporting framework is the Carbon Disclosure Project (CDP), which focuses specifically on the measurement and reduction of carbon emissions. For warehouses, reporting to the CDP provides transparency about their carbon footprint and helps them set measurable goals for emissions reduction.

ISO 14001: Many warehouses may choose to report their sustainability efforts through ISO 14001 certification, which focuses on environmental management systems. ISO 14001 certification is a globally recognized standard that demonstrates an organization's commitment to reducing its environmental impact. By adhering to this standard, warehouses can ensure they are continuously improving their sustainability performance and providing measurable results.

The Role of Transparency in Building Stakeholder Trust

Transparency goes hand-in-hand with accountability. When warehouses share detailed, accurate reports on their sustainability practices, it builds trust among stakeholders. Transparency also enables stakeholders to hold the organization accountable for its claims and to track progress over time.

Employee and Stakeholder Engagement: Transparent sustainability reporting also serves as a tool for internal engagement. Employees who are informed about the company's environmental goals and progress are more likely to feel motivated and engaged in achieving those objectives. Similarly, external stakeholders—such as investors, customers, and local communities—are more likely to support a company that is open about its challenges and successes in sustainability.

Building Consumer Trust and Loyalty: For customers, transparency is a vital factor in making purchasing decisions. Many consumers today are more concerned about the environmental and social practices of the companies they support. By publicly sharing sustainability efforts, warehouses can strengthen customer loyalty and attract new business from consumers who prioritize green practices.

Investor Confidence: Investors are increasingly looking to support companies that demonstrate strong environmental, social, and governance (ESG) practices. Transparent sustainability reporting gives investors confidence that a warehouse is managing its environmental risks, complying with regulations, and investing in future growth through sustainable practices.

Communicating Progress and Challenges

While transparency involves reporting successes, it also means being honest about challenges. No organization is perfect, and sustainability efforts often face hurdles along the way. Being transparent about these challenges—whether it's struggling to meet emissions targets or facing supply chain disruptions—can actually enhance credibility. By acknowledging difficulties and outlining strategies for improvement, warehouses can demonstrate their commitment to continuous progress.

Annual Sustainability Reports: Many warehouses choose to publish annual sustainability reports that include data on key performance indicators (KPIs) such as energy use, waste diversion rates, and carbon emissions. These reports often include case studies, testimonials, and project summaries that show how specific initiatives have led to tangible environmental benefits. By regularly publishing these reports, warehouses can track their progress year-over-year and communicate this to stakeholders.

Interactive Platforms for Stakeholder Engagement: With the rise of digital communication tools, some warehouses are adopting interactive platforms to keep stakeholders informed about sustainability efforts. These platforms allow customers, employees, and community members to access real-time data on warehouse performance, submit feedback, and engage directly with sustainability teams. This level of engagement fosters transparency and builds a sense of community around shared sustainability goals.

Effective community and stakeholder engagement is essential for warehouses aiming to integrate sustainability into their operations. By partnering with local communities and providing transparency in sustainability reporting, warehouses can build trust, foster goodwill, and enhance their social license to operate. These efforts not only contribute to the warehouse's environmental goals but also strengthen its relationship with the surrounding community, employees, and other stakeholders. Ultimately, sustainable warehousing is about fostering collaboration, maintaining open communication, and continuously striving to minimize the negative impacts of operations while maximizing positive contributions to society and the environment.

Part VII: Circular Economy and Warehousing

Adopting Circular Economy Principles

The concept of a circular economy is gaining traction across industries, including warehousing, as businesses increasingly seek ways to minimize waste and maximize resource efficiency. Unlike the traditional linear economy, which follows a "take-make-dispose" model, the circular economy is designed to close the loop of product lifecycles through greater resource efficiency, reuse, recycling, and remanufacturing. In the context of warehousing, adopting circular economy principles can significantly reduce environmental impact, optimize operational efficiency, and contribute to the long-term sustainability of the supply chain.

This chapter explores how warehouses can adopt circular economy principles, focusing on closing the loop in warehouse operations, reverse logistics, and establishing effective recycling systems.

1. Closing the Loop in Warehouse Operations

The first step towards implementing a circular economy in warehouse operations is to fundamentally rethink how materials, products, and resources are handled throughout the lifecycle. Closing the loop involves creating systems where resources, waste, and products are continually reused, refurbished, or recycled, rather than disposed of after their initial use.

Sustainable Packaging Solutions

One of the most significant areas where circular economy principles can be applied in warehousing is through sustainable packaging. Packaging materials, such as plastic, cardboard, and Styrofoam, have long been a major source of waste. By transitioning to eco-friendly, reusable, or recyclable packaging solutions, warehouses can reduce the volume of packaging waste they generate, making a substantial contribution to the circular economy.

Reusable Packaging: Introducing reusable packaging solutions, such as plastic crates, bulk containers, or palletized shipments, can reduce the need for single-use packaging materials. For example, products that are shipped in bulk can be transported in reusable containers that are returned after delivery, cleaned, and reused for future shipments. This approach drastically reduces the environmental impact associated with packaging production and disposal.

Composting and Biodegradable Materials: In addition to reusable containers, warehouses can adopt biodegradable or compostable materials for packaging. For instance, mushroom-based packaging, cornstarch, and other plant-derived alternatives offer an eco-friendly alternative to traditional plastic packaging. These materials break down naturally, causing less environmental harm when discarded. Warehouses can establish dedicated systems to compost organic waste, creating nutrient-rich soil for local agricultural or landscaping projects.

Packaging Design and Reduction: Another strategy for closing the loop in warehousing is through smarter packaging design that minimizes material use without compromising product protection. For instance, minimizing the size and weight of packaging can help reduce waste and improve the efficiency of warehouse space. Additionally, optimizing package design to fit the products precisely can reduce the need for excessive filler materials, contributing to sustainability efforts.

Reducing Waste in the Supply Chain

Warehouses are often at the intersection of goods moving through the supply chain, and waste reduction at this stage can significantly influence overall efficiency. In the circular economy model, reducing waste involves minimizing the loss of products and materials during transportation, storage, and handling.

Inventory Optimization: By adopting just-in-time (JIT) inventory techniques or other inventory management systems like ABC analysis, warehouses can minimize the amount of unsold or excess stock that might eventually be discarded. Overstocking is a significant contributor to waste in warehouses, as unsold or outdated products often need to be disposed of. Efficient inventory management helps ensure that products move in and out of the warehouse quickly and are used before they reach the end of their useful life.

Energy and Resource Efficiency: Closing the loop also means using resources, including energy, water, and raw materials, more efficiently. Energy-efficient lighting, renewable energy sources, and eco-friendly building materials are all part of reducing the resource footprint of warehouse operations. By employing energy-efficient machinery and optimized operational strategies, warehouses can reduce their overall resource consumption, contributing to both environmental sustainability and cost savings.

2. Reverse Logistics and Recycling Systems

Reverse logistics refers to the process of moving goods from their final destination back to the warehouse or manufacturer for reuse, recycling, remanufacturing, or disposal. In a circular economy, reverse logistics plays a crucial role in closing the loop by ensuring that materials and products are not wasted after their first use.

Reverse Logistics in Warehousing

Reverse logistics has grown in importance as a strategic element of supply chain management, particularly as consumer demand for sustainable products and services increases. Warehouses play a vital role in facilitating reverse logistics by handling returns, repairs, refurbishments, and recycling processes.

Product Returns: In industries such as e-commerce, fashion, and electronics, product returns are common, and managing these returns in a sustainable manner is essential. Instead of disposing of returned products, warehouses can develop systems for inspecting, repairing, or refurbishing them for resale, thus giving them a second life. This process not only reduces waste but also creates an opportunity to recover valuable resources, such as raw materials and components, that can be reused in manufacturing.

Returnable and Reusable Containers: A common practice in reverse logistics is the use of returnable containers or pallets.

These containers, often made of durable plastic or metal, can be returned to the warehouse after delivering goods and used for future shipments. Implementing systems that track these reusable containers and ensure they are returned in a timely manner reduces the need for single-use packaging and lowers the warehouse's overall environmental footprint.

Take-back Programs: For certain product categories—such as electronics, batteries, or appliances—warehouses can implement take-back programs. These programs encourage consumers or businesses to return used products for proper recycling or disposal, preventing them from ending up in landfills. The warehouse can then handle the logistics of disassembling, recycling, or repurposing the materials for use in new products.

Establishing Effective Recycling Systems

Warehouses, by nature, generate large amounts of waste—whether it's packaging materials, obsolete products, or by-products of operations. Recycling is an essential component of a circular economy, and warehouses can implement efficient systems to handle and recycle waste materials, diverting them from landfills.

Segregating Waste Streams: Effective recycling begins with sorting waste at the source. Warehouses can implement systems to separate materials such as cardboard, plastics, metals, and paper so that they can be sent to the appropriate recycling facilities. By training employees and providing the necessary infrastructure—such as labeled bins and designated recycling areas—warehouses can streamline the recycling process and ensure that materials are properly processed.

Recycling Packaging Materials: A significant portion of warehouse waste comes from packaging materials. Cardboard, plastic wrap, and foam are commonly used in packaging products for storage and shipment. Many of these materials are recyclable and can be processed into new products. For example, cardboard can be shredded and used as packing material, while plastics can be melted down and repurposed into new packaging or building materials.

E-Waste Recycling: In warehouses dealing with electronics or electrical goods, the recycling of electronic waste (e-waste) is an essential part of circular economy practices. E-waste, including old computers, batteries, and defective products, contains valuable metals and components that can be extracted and reused. Implementing e-waste recycling programs in collaboration with specialized recycling companies ensures that these materials are properly handled and do not contribute to environmental harm.

Partnerships with Recycling Facilities: To ensure that recycling efforts are effective, warehouses can establish relationships with certified recycling facilities. These facilities are equipped to handle specific waste streams, such as hazardous materials or specialized packaging, ensuring that materials are processed responsibly and efficiently.

3. The Circular Economy in the Broader Supply Chain

The integration of circular economy principles in warehousing must extend beyond individual warehouse operations to encompass the entire supply chain. By working collaboratively with suppliers, manufacturers, and other stakeholders, warehouses can help drive circularity throughout the product lifecycle, from raw material extraction to end-of-life product disposal.

Collaborating with Suppliers: Warehouses can engage with suppliers to reduce waste at the source. For example, they can work with manufacturers to design products with a longer lifespan, more sustainable packaging, or materials that are easier to recycle. By incorporating circular principles into the procurement process, warehouses can help create a more sustainable supply chain from the very beginning.

Design for Disassembly and Recycling: One important consideration for warehouses engaged in the circular economy is working with manufacturers to ensure that products are designed for easy disassembly and recycling. Products with modular designs or that use fewer non-recyclable materials can be more easily refurbished, reused, or recycled at the end of their life.

Collaborative Waste Management: Instead of working in silos, warehouses can collaborate with other companies and industries to establish shared recycling initiatives. For example, several warehouses in a region can jointly operate recycling facilities or share transportation resources for recycling efforts, reducing overall costs and increasing the efficiency of waste management.

Adopting circular economy principles in warehousing involves a holistic approach that touches every part of the operation. By focusing on closing the loop through sustainable packaging, reducing waste, and implementing reverse logistics and recycling systems, warehouses can contribute to a more sustainable future. However, the transition to a circular economy requires collaboration across the entire supply chain, from suppliers to consumers, ensuring that materials and products are continually reused and recycled. With increasing pressure to adopt sustainable practices and reduce environmental impact, warehouses that embrace circular economy principles will not only reduce their ecological footprint but also position themselves as leaders in the green economy, benefiting both their bottom line and the planet.

Repair, Refurbish, and Resell Initiatives

In the context of sustainable warehousing and the broader circular economy, the repair, refurbishment, and resale of goods represents a crucial strategy for minimizing waste, extending the lifecycle of products, and creating value from previously used items. By implementing these initiatives, warehouses can actively contribute to the reduction of waste and the promotion of sustainability, while also opening up new revenue streams through the resale of refurbished goods.

This chapter explores how warehouses can integrate repair, refurbishment, and resale initiatives into their operations to not only enhance sustainability but also create a competitive advantage. It discusses the strategies for handling returns sustainably and the value created through refurbished goods.

1. Strategies for Handling Returns Sustainably

Returns management is an inevitable part of warehouse operations, particularly in sectors such as e-commerce, fashion, and electronics. However, instead of treating returns as waste, warehouses can embrace sustainable approaches to manage returned items in ways that align with circular economy principles. This process is commonly referred to as reverse logistics, which involves the movement of goods from the consumer back to the warehouse for reuse, recycling, or disposal.

Optimizing the Returns Process

The first step in handling returns sustainably is creating an optimized reverse logistics process that minimizes waste and reduces the environmental impact. Effective returns management systems are essential in determining whether returned goods should be refurbished, repaired, recycled, or disposed of.

Inspection and Assessment: When returned goods arrive at the warehouse, they must be carefully inspected to assess their condition. This inspection should not only check for damages but also determine the potential for repair, refurbishment, or resale. Products that are only slightly damaged or have minor defects can often be restored to a usable condition, whereas products that are irreparably damaged should be diverted for recycling or responsible disposal.

Clear Return Policies: Clear and transparent return policies play a vital role in sustainability. For example, offering customers incentives to keep items rather than returning them, such as a discount on a future purchase, can significantly reduce return rates. Alternatively, encouraging customers to choose the correct size or model in the first place by providing detailed product descriptions, size guides, and reviews can minimize the likelihood of returns.

Repair and Refurbishment Facilities: Warehouses that handle returns sustainably should ideally have designated areas or partnerships with external repair facilities that can repair or refurbish returned products. For example, in the electronics industry, returned gadgets that have minor defects can be refurbished and resold, helping to reduce the overall number of new products being manufactured.

Packaging for Returns

Sustainable packaging is another critical element in reverse logistics. Just as warehouses aim to reduce packaging waste in the outbound logistics process, they should ensure that returned products are repackaged using eco-friendly or reusable materials. If a product is being returned for repair or refurbishment, the packaging should be reusable, ensuring it can be used again for future shipments or returns. This reduces the need for single-use packaging and minimizes the warehouse's environmental impact.

Collaborating with Partners

Warehouses can also collaborate with manufacturers, third-party logistics providers, and specialized refurbishment centers to ensure that returned goods are effectively repaired, refurbished, or recycled. By partnering with these entities, warehouses can leverage expertise and resources to handle returns in a more sustainable and efficient manner.

2. Creating Value Through Refurbished Goods

Refurbishing returned goods is a powerful strategy that warehouses can employ to extract additional value from products that would otherwise be discarded. By repairing and restoring products to their original functionality, warehouses can create new revenue streams, reduce waste, and support the broader goals of a circular economy.

The Refurbishment Process

Refurbishment involves taking a returned or damaged product, repairing it, and restoring it to a condition that is comparable to new. The extent of the refurbishment process can vary depending on the product type, condition of the returned item, and the warehouse's capacity. In many cases, refurbishing can involve a thorough cleaning, repairing of broken or defective parts, re-packaging, and ensuring that the product meets the manufacturer's standards.

Electronics Refurbishment: Electronics is one of the largest industries where refurbished goods are in high demand. Items such as smartphones, computers, and household appliances are often returned due to minor issues that can be repaired. For instance, a phone with a cracked screen or a malfunctioning charging port can be refurbished and resold, providing consumers with a more affordable option while reducing e-waste.

Furniture and Home Goods: In industries like furniture or home goods, products can often be refurbished by fixing cosmetic damage, reupholstering, or reassembling damaged parts. These items, once refurbished, are sold at a lower price point, creating a more sustainable market for consumers who may not be able to afford new items.

Clothing and Fashion: Refurbishing extends to the fashion industry as well, where returned or slightly damaged clothing can be repaired, cleaned, or altered and then resold as pre-owned or upcycled items. These efforts reduce textile waste, promote more sustainable fashion, and support the growing market for second-hand goods.

Economic Value of Refurbished Goods

Refurbished goods offer considerable economic value to both the warehouse and the consumer. For warehouses, reselling refurbished goods can significantly increase profit margins, especially when the original product would otherwise have been discarded. Refurbishment typically costs a fraction of the price of manufacturing a new product, which translates into higher profit margins from refurbished sales.

Cost-Effective Operations: By adopting refurbishment strategies, warehouses can maximize the lifespan of returned products. Instead of disposing of products that are still usable, warehouses can invest in relatively low-cost repairs and restoration to generate significant returns. For example, a returned electronic device with a minor defect might cost a warehouse $20 to repair, but the same device could be resold for $100 or more, generating a substantial profit.

Affordability for Consumers: Refurbished goods provide an affordable alternative for consumers who might not be able to purchase new items. Many consumers are willing to buy refurbished products if they are guaranteed to be as good as new or come with a warranty. The resale of refurbished goods helps meet consumer demand for lower-cost, high-quality products while promoting a circular economy.

Environmental Impact of Refurbished Goods

The environmental impact of refurbishing goods is profound. By extending the life cycle of products, warehouses reduce the demand for new raw materials and manufacturing, which in turn decreases energy consumption and greenhouse gas emissions. Additionally, refurbishing prevents products from ending up in landfills, helping to divert waste and promote recycling. In industries such as electronics, where e-waste is a growing concern, refurbishment plays a critical role in reducing the ecological footprint of the sector.

E-Waste Reduction: Electronic waste is one of the fastest-growing types of waste globally. By refurbishing and reselling electronic products, warehouses contribute to reducing the amount of e-waste that ends up in landfills, where it can release harmful toxins into the environment. Refurbishing electronics also recovers valuable materials, such as precious metals, that can be reused in future production.

Decreasing Raw Material Demand: Every time a product is refurbished and resold, it reduces the need for raw materials to manufacture a new product. For example, the metals, plastics, and components used in electronics and other goods can be reused, limiting the environmental costs associated with extracting and processing these materials.

3. Customer Perception and Branding

Beyond the direct environmental and economic benefits, repair, refurbish, and resell initiatives offer warehouses the opportunity to build stronger relationships with environmentally conscious consumers. The increasing demand for sustainability in products has led many consumers to prioritize businesses that offer environmentally friendly options.

Eco-friendly Branding: Warehouses that actively engage in refurbishing and reselling products can leverage this initiative in their marketing and branding efforts. By promoting the sale of refurbished goods, businesses can position themselves as environmentally responsible, attracting customers who are committed to sustainability.

Customer Trust and Loyalty: Offering refurbished products not only aligns with the values of sustainability but can also build trust and loyalty among consumers. Customers are more likely to support businesses that demonstrate a commitment to reducing their environmental impact, and providing access to high-quality refurbished goods is one way warehouses can strengthen customer relationships.

Repair, refurbish, and resell initiatives represent an essential aspect of sustainable warehousing, offering substantial environmental, economic, and social benefits. By implementing effective strategies for handling returns and creating value through refurbished goods, warehouses can reduce waste, lower costs, and contribute to a more sustainable and circular economy. Moreover, as consumers become increasingly focused on sustainability, warehouses that embrace these initiatives are well-positioned to strengthen their market position, enhance customer loyalty, and promote a greener future.

Part VIII: Future of Sustainable Warehousing

Emerging Trends in Sustainable Warehousing

As sustainability continues to take center stage in business strategies worldwide, the warehousing and logistics industries are also shifting toward greener practices. The future of sustainable warehousing will be shaped by emerging trends and innovations that focus not only on improving operational efficiencies but also on reducing environmental impacts. This chapter will explore the key trends in green innovations in construction and operations, as well as the technologies that will shape the future of green warehousing.

Emerging Trends in Sustainable Warehousing

1. Green Innovations in Construction and Operations

The demand for sustainable warehouses is growing as companies and consumers alike are increasingly aware of the environmental impact of traditional logistics operations. Green innovations in both the construction of warehouses and their day-to-day operations are transforming the industry and creating a pathway to more energy-efficient, resource-conserving facilities.

Energy-Efficient Building Designs: One of the most significant trends in warehouse construction is the integration of energy-efficient building designs. Architects and construction engineers are working toward designing warehouses that consume less energy, use renewable resources, and have smaller carbon footprints. This includes using high-performance insulation materials, energy-efficient windows, and state-of-the-art heating, ventilation, and air conditioning (HVAC) systems. A growing trend is the installation of green roofs and living walls that not only improve insulation but also reduce stormwater runoff, support biodiversity, and contribute to cleaner air.

Net-Zero and Carbon-Neutral Buildings: Another emerging trend in warehouse construction is the focus on net-zero energy and carbon-neutral buildings. These facilities aim to offset their energy consumption through renewable energy sources such as solar panels and wind turbines, effectively reducing their carbon footprint to zero. By integrating renewable energy systems into the building design, warehouses can lower operational costs and become energy-independent. Several major logistics companies are already investing in net-zero warehouse facilities to demonstrate their commitment to environmental sustainability.

Modular and Prefabricated Construction: Prefabricated and modular construction methods are gaining traction in warehouse design as a way to reduce waste and improve efficiency. These methods allow for quicker construction times, better quality control, and less material waste compared to traditional building practices. Modular construction also allows for easy expansion and reconfiguration of warehouse spaces, making it a flexible and scalable solution for growing companies. This trend supports the circular economy by reducing the need for new raw materials and minimizing construction debris.

Sustainable Materials: The use of sustainable building materials is also on the rise. Recycled materials such as steel, reclaimed wood, and recycled concrete are increasingly being used in the construction of warehouses. These materials not only reduce the demand for new raw materials but also help divert waste from landfills. The adoption of low-VOC paints and finishes, as well as sustainable flooring options like bamboo or cork, further contributes to healthier indoor environments and reduces the environmental impact of warehouse construction.

2. Green Operations and Eco-Friendly Practices

Beyond the construction phase, many warehouses are focusing on improving the sustainability of their daily operations. The ongoing optimization of energy consumption, waste management, and material handling processes is key to reducing the environmental impact of warehousing operations.

Smart Lighting and HVAC Systems: One of the most impactful green innovations in warehouse operations is the use of smart lighting and HVAC systems. By integrating sensors and automated controls, warehouses can optimize lighting and temperature based on occupancy and weather conditions. For example, motion sensors can turn lights off in areas that are not in use, while thermostats can adjust temperature settings to reduce heating and cooling costs when the warehouse is not fully operational. These systems not only reduce energy consumption but also improve the comfort of warehouse workers.

Warehouse Automation: The increasing use of automation in warehouses is another significant trend. Automated systems such as robotic pickers, automated guided vehicles (AGVs), and conveyor systems are improving operational efficiency while reducing the need for energy-intensive human labor. Automation can optimize the flow of materials, reduce idle time, and decrease energy consumption by minimizing excess movement. Furthermore, automated systems can be integrated with energy-efficient practices to ensure that operations are optimized for sustainability.

Green Packaging: Sustainable packaging solutions are becoming a critical focus for warehouses, especially in industries such as e-commerce and retail. Eco-friendly packaging materials, such as biodegradable plastic alternatives, recycled cardboard, and reusable packaging, help reduce the volume of packaging waste generated by warehouse operations. In addition to reducing environmental harm, green packaging practices can also contribute to cost savings by lowering material costs and improving supply chain efficiency. Many companies are adopting a packaging take-back model, where customers can return packaging for reuse or recycling.

Waste Reduction and Recycling Programs: As part of their commitment to sustainability, many warehouses are implementing more effective waste reduction and recycling programs. This includes segregating recyclable materials, such as plastics, paper, and metals, and partnering with recycling facilities to ensure that materials are reused in the manufacturing process. In some cases, warehouses are even implementing composting programs for organic waste, which can be repurposed for local agriculture or energy production.

Future Technologies Shaping Green Warehousing

1. Artificial Intelligence (AI) and Machine Learning

AI and machine learning technologies have the potential to revolutionize sustainable warehousing by improving decision-making processes and optimizing resource usage. These technologies can be leveraged to predict demand, optimize inventory levels, and automate energy-efficient practices in real-time.

Predictive Analytics for Resource Management: AI-powered predictive analytics can help warehouses forecast energy demand and adjust operations accordingly. For instance, machine learning algorithms can analyze weather patterns, operational data, and historical energy usage to predict fluctuations in energy demand. Based on this data, warehouses can adjust lighting, HVAC systems, and production schedules to minimize energy waste and reduce consumption.

Optimized Inventory Management: AI can also enhance inventory management systems, reducing overstocking and minimizing waste. By analyzing customer behavior and purchasing patterns, AI algorithms can predict the optimal inventory levels needed to meet demand without overproduction. This helps reduce the carbon footprint associated with excess manufacturing and transportation.

2. Internet of Things (IoT)

The Internet of Things (IoT) is another key technology shaping the future of sustainable warehousing. IoT devices, such as sensors and connected equipment, enable warehouses to collect real-time data on energy consumption, environmental conditions, and equipment performance. This data can be used to optimize warehouse operations and reduce energy usage.

Smart Energy Management Systems: IoT-enabled energy management systems allow warehouses to monitor and control their energy usage in real time. Sensors can track the performance of lighting, HVAC systems, and machinery, and provide insights into potential inefficiencies or opportunities for energy savings. By integrating these IoT devices with automation systems, warehouses can proactively adjust their energy consumption to optimize efficiency and reduce waste.

Smart Inventory and Warehouse Management: IoT is also transforming inventory and warehouse management by providing real-time visibility into stock levels, locations, and conditions. By tracking inventory with RFID tags and connected devices, warehouses can optimize storage space, reduce the need for overstocking, and minimize product spoilage. This leads to more efficient operations and less waste.

3. Blockchain Technology

Blockchain technology is emerging as a powerful tool for improving transparency and traceability in supply chains, including warehousing. By creating an immutable ledger of transactions, blockchain can help ensure that sustainable practices are being followed at every stage of the supply chain.

Sustainable Sourcing and Provenance Tracking: Blockchain enables warehouses to track the provenance of products and raw materials, ensuring that they are sourced sustainably. This transparency can help verify that suppliers adhere to ethical and environmental standards, improving accountability across the supply chain. Furthermore, blockchain can help prevent fraud and counterfeiting, ensuring that sustainable goods are accurately labeled and distributed.

Energy and Carbon Tracking: Blockchain can also be used to track energy usage and carbon emissions within warehouses. By integrating IoT sensors and energy management systems with blockchain, warehouses can create a transparent record of their environmental impact. This data can be shared with stakeholders, regulators, and consumers to demonstrate the warehouse's commitment to sustainability.

The future of sustainable warehousing will be shaped by an ongoing commitment to green innovations in construction, operations, and technology. As warehouses adopt energy-efficient building designs, embrace automation and AI, and integrate renewable energy solutions, they will not only reduce their environmental impact but also enhance operational efficiency and profitability. The increasing use of technologies like IoT, blockchain, and AI will further drive sustainability in warehouse operations, creating a more transparent, energy-efficient, and circular supply chain.

In the coming years, the integration of sustainability in warehousing will no longer be a competitive advantage but a necessity for staying relevant in an increasingly environmentally conscious market. By embracing these trends and technologies, warehouses can create a positive impact on both the environment and their bottom line, ensuring that they remain resilient and profitable in a sustainable future.

Resilience and Adaptability in Warehousing

As the world experiences the increasing effects of climate change, industries worldwide are being called to rethink their strategies for risk management, business continuity, and environmental responsibility. For warehousing, this means preparing for climate change impacts, building disaster-resilient infrastructures, and creating operational systems that can adapt to changing environmental conditions. This chapter explores how warehouses can improve their resilience and adaptability, focusing on the critical steps needed to prepare for climate change, ensure continuity during natural disasters, and integrate long-term sustainability into warehouse design and operations.

1. Preparing for Climate Change Impacts

Climate change is no longer a distant concern—it is a present reality that affects all industries, particularly warehousing and logistics. Rising temperatures, extreme weather events, and shifts in precipitation patterns can have profound implications on warehouse operations, supply chain reliability, and infrastructure longevity. As such, warehouses must adapt to these changing conditions to minimize risks and ensure long-term sustainability.

a. Vulnerabilities of Warehouses to Climate Change

Warehouses are exposed to a range of environmental hazards brought on by climate change, including:

Extreme Weather Events: Flooding, hurricanes, tornadoes, heatwaves, and storms can damage infrastructure, disrupt supply chains, and delay deliveries. These events can cause power outages, impair road transport, and lead to inventory loss or spoilage, especially in areas where warehouses store perishable goods.

Temperature Extremes: Rising global temperatures and fluctuating seasonal temperatures can affect the efficiency of warehouse operations. For example, temperature-sensitive products such as pharmaceuticals, chemicals, and foodstuffs require consistent storage conditions, and extreme temperatures can cause spoilage or damage.

Rising Sea Levels: Warehouses located in coastal areas or flood-prone regions are particularly vulnerable to rising sea levels and flooding. These areas face a higher risk of infrastructure damage, which can disrupt the entire supply chain.

Water Scarcity: In regions where climate change leads to prolonged droughts, water shortages can severely affect warehouse operations, especially in industries reliant on water for cleaning, cooling, or production processes.

b. Adapting to Climate Change

To prepare for these impacts, warehouses must implement strategies that reduce vulnerability and enhance operational resilience. These strategies include:

Site Selection and Infrastructure Resilience: When selecting sites for new warehouses, companies must consider climate risks such as flood zones, extreme heat, and potential impacts from rising sea levels. Warehouses should be designed and built to withstand severe weather, using durable materials and structural reinforcements to minimize damage during extreme events. Elevated warehouses, for instance, can help prevent flood damage in flood-prone regions.

Climate-Resilient Infrastructure: Investing in climate-resilient building materials and structures is crucial for mitigating the effects of extreme weather. These might include high-strength concrete, waterproof coatings, reinforced roofing, and windows designed to resist high winds. Moreover, warehouses in areas prone to wildfires can use fire-resistant materials to protect goods and assets. Proper drainage systems and waterproofing techniques also prevent flooding from heavy rains, while green roofs and walls help regulate indoor temperatures.

Renewable Energy and Off-Grid Solutions: In anticipation of disruptions to the power grid due to storms or heatwaves, warehouses are increasingly investing in renewable energy sources such as solar panels, wind turbines, or geothermal heating and cooling systems. These sustainable energy systems not only contribute to environmental goals but also ensure energy independence during outages, providing a reliable power source even in the event of a disaster.

Resilient Supply Chain Networks: A robust, adaptable supply chain is crucial to mitigating the impacts of climate change. Warehouses can build resilience into their supply chains by diversifying suppliers, establishing alternative transportation routes, and incorporating flexibility into inventory management. By diversifying sources and routes, warehouses are better prepared for disruptions caused by natural disasters, allowing them to maintain supply chain operations and reduce downtime.

2. Building Disaster-Resilient Warehouses

Disaster resilience goes beyond preparing for climate-related challenges—it also involves ensuring that warehouses can continue operations during and after a disaster. Resilient warehouses are equipped with systems, technologies, and strategies that help mitigate risks, respond to emergencies, and recover quickly after disruptions.

a. Disaster-Resilient Design Principles

The physical design of a warehouse plays a key role in disaster resilience. Several design principles can be integrated into warehouse planning to ensure that they are capable of withstanding extreme events:

Structural Integrity and Load-Bearing Capacity: Warehouses in hurricane or earthquake-prone areas should be designed with reinforced structures to withstand strong winds and seismic activity. For instance, flexible building frames and high-strength concrete can be used to reduce the risk of structural collapse during an earthquake. Buildings should also be built to handle the weight of heavy loads, ensuring that racking systems, machinery, and goods can remain stable in extreme conditions.

Flood Mitigation: Warehouses located in flood-prone areas must be built to prevent or mitigate flood damage. Elevated flooring, flood barriers, and waterproof seals on doors and windows can reduce the risk of water entering the building. Additionally, incorporating rainwater harvesting systems and using permeable materials for the exterior of the warehouse can help absorb excess water during heavy rainfall and minimize the risk of flooding.

Fire-Resistant Materials and Systems: In areas prone to wildfires or extreme heat, warehouses must include fire-resistant materials in their construction. This includes fire-resistant roofing, insulation, walls, and doors. Warehouses should also install automatic sprinkler systems, fire alarms, and firebreaks to contain and manage fires effectively.

Climate-Controlled Storage Areas: For temperature-sensitive goods, disaster-resilient warehouses must have climate-controlled storage zones equipped with backup power systems. These areas ensure that goods such as perishable food, pharmaceuticals, and electronics remain at optimal conditions, even if power systems are disrupted by extreme weather events.

b. Disaster Recovery Plans and Business Continuity

Resilience in warehousing also involves having effective disaster recovery plans and business continuity strategies. These plans should focus on maintaining operational capacity, safeguarding inventory, and enabling a quick recovery after a disaster.

Emergency Response Protocols: A comprehensive disaster response plan should outline protocols for warehouse personnel in case of an emergency, such as evacuation procedures, emergency supplies, and immediate actions to protect the warehouse from damage. A well-trained workforce will be crucial in reducing risks and ensuring smooth recovery.

Redundant Systems and Backups: To ensure business continuity, disaster-resilient warehouses often incorporate redundant systems, such as backup power generators, redundant data storage, and network backups. In the event of a power outage or system failure, these backups help prevent disruptions to warehouse operations and protect vital systems.

Supply Chain Recovery Plans: A disaster-resilient warehouse is not only concerned with its own infrastructure but also with its role in the broader supply chain. Recovery plans should include provisions for maintaining inventory levels, finding alternate suppliers, and using backup transport routes. This enables warehouses to continue fulfilling customer orders and receiving new shipments, even when disruptions occur in other parts of the supply chain.

c. Technology Integration for Disaster Resilience

Incorporating advanced technologies is another critical element of building disaster-resilient warehouses. The use of Internet of Things (IoT) devices, real-time data analytics, and automation can enhance operational resilience by enabling warehouses to monitor and respond to potential threats more effectively.

Real-Time Monitoring Systems: IoT sensors can monitor critical factors such as temperature, humidity, air quality, and structural integrity in real-time. These systems can alert warehouse managers to any signs of impending damage, such as water leakage or temperature deviations, allowing for timely intervention before a disaster escalates.

Automated Shutdown Systems: In the event of a disaster, automated systems can help mitigate damage by performing automatic shutdowns of critical systems. For instance, in the case of an earthquake, automated systems could disable machinery and close off access to hazardous areas, reducing the risk of further damage or injury.

Predictive Analytics for Risk Management: Using data analytics, warehouses can assess the likelihood of potential disasters based on historical data and predictive models. This allows managers to better prepare for extreme events by adjusting inventory levels, optimizing warehouse layouts, and ensuring the right resources are in place to handle various disaster scenarios.

Building resilience and adaptability into warehousing operations is not just a reaction to climate change—it is a proactive approach to ensuring long-term business continuity and environmental sustainability. As climate-related risks continue to grow, the warehousing industry must adopt climate-resilient designs, disaster-preparedness strategies, and cutting-edge technologies to safeguard infrastructure, maintain operational capacity, and support the supply chain during and after natural disasters.

By investing in disaster-resilient infrastructure, adopting flexible and adaptive systems, and integrating green technologies, warehouses can reduce their vulnerability to climate change, minimize operational disruptions, and emerge stronger in the face of adversity. These efforts not only ensure the survival of warehouse operations in challenging times but also contribute to the creation of a more sustainable, resilient supply chain for the future.

Integrating ESG Goals in Warehousing

The warehousing sector, as a vital part of global supply chains, is increasingly being called upon to align with Environmental, Social, and Governance (ESG) frameworks. These frameworks are designed to guide companies in managing the risks and opportunities associated with environmental, social, and governance issues. By integrating ESG goals into warehousing operations, companies can not only reduce their environmental footprint but also enhance their social impact, improve governance practices, and bolster their reputation in the marketplace. This chapter will explore how ESG goals can be effectively integrated into warehousing operations, and the potential benefits and challenges associated with such integration.

1. Linking Warehousing to ESG Frameworks

ESG frameworks consist of three main pillars: environmental, social, and governance. These principles guide businesses in making responsible and sustainable decisions that have a positive impact on society, the environment, and the long-term success of the organization. Warehousing operations, which often involve large-scale storage, material handling, transportation, and energy-intensive activities, play a significant role in achieving ESG goals.

a. Environmental Goals in Warehousing

The environmental aspect of ESG focuses on how a company manages its impact on the planet, including its carbon footprint, energy consumption, waste management, and resource use. Warehouses, as energy-intensive operations with high emissions, need to adopt strategies that minimize their environmental impact and contribute to the global push for sustainability.

Energy Efficiency and Green Building Design: One of the primary environmental goals in warehousing is energy efficiency. Implementing energy-efficient technologies, such as LED lighting, energy-efficient HVAC systems, and renewable energy sources like solar panels, can significantly reduce a warehouse's energy consumption. Green building certifications like LEED (Leadership in Energy and Environmental Design) or BREEAM (Building Research Establishment Environmental Assessment Method) offer guidelines for designing energy-efficient and environmentally responsible warehouse buildings.

Reducing Carbon Footprint: Reducing greenhouse gas emissions is central to many ESG strategies. Warehouses can reduce their carbon footprint by adopting sustainable transportation practices (e.g., using electric vehicles, optimizing delivery routes), improving the efficiency of material handling equipment, and investing in technologies like warehouse automation and IoT, which optimize energy use and minimize waste.

Waste Management and Circular Economy: Sustainable warehouses should prioritize waste reduction by adopting a circular economy approach. This includes reducing, reusing, and recycling materials, managing packaging waste sustainably, and setting up systems for responsible disposal of hazardous materials. By implementing robust recycling programs, warehouses can contribute to the reduction of landfill waste and support a more circular flow of resources.

b. Social Goals in Warehousing

The social aspect of ESG is concerned with a company's impact on its employees, customers, and communities. For warehousing, this includes providing safe and fair working conditions, fostering a culture of diversity and inclusion, and ensuring that the warehouse's operations do not harm the community or society at large.

Worker Safety and Well-Being: Warehouses are high-risk environments, with heavy machinery, forklifts, and high shelves. Prioritizing the safety and well-being of employees is critical for meeting social sustainability goals. This includes implementing comprehensive safety training, using automated systems to reduce human error, and ensuring that warehouses comply with Occupational Safety and Health Administration (OSHA) standards. Offering health benefits, competitive wages, and promoting mental and physical well-being are also essential components of fostering a socially responsible work environment.

Fair Labor Practices and Employee Engagement: Social goals in warehousing also focus on labor practices. This includes paying fair wages, providing equal opportunities for workers regardless of race, gender, or background, and offering benefits such as healthcare, paid leave, and job security. Additionally, employee engagement is crucial; fostering a culture of respect, innovation, and inclusivity helps to ensure the workforce is motivated, productive, and aligned with the company's values.

Community Impact: Beyond the warehouse floor, businesses are increasingly expected to support and engage with the communities in which they operate. Warehouses can make a positive social impact by participating in local initiatives, supporting charities, or engaging in community outreach programs. They can also minimize the negative impact of their operations on local communities by ensuring their environmental practices do not contribute to pollution or degradation of local resources.

c. Governance Goals in Warehousing

Governance refers to the systems, processes, and policies that ensure a company is managed responsibly and ethically. For warehousing, strong governance practices help ensure compliance with laws and regulations, transparency in operations, and ethical decision-making throughout the supply chain.

Ethical Sourcing and Supply Chain Transparency: In the context of warehousing, governance goals include ensuring that goods are sourced responsibly and that the supply chain adheres to ethical standards. This involves working with suppliers who uphold ESG principles and ensuring that products stored in warehouses are not associated with human rights abuses or environmental harm. Warehouses can also improve transparency by disclosing their environmental and social practices in annual sustainability reports, allowing stakeholders to track the company's progress.

Data Protection and Security: As warehouses increasingly adopt digital technologies such as IoT devices, Warehouse Management Systems (WMS), and robotics, they must ensure strong governance around data protection and cybersecurity. Protecting customer and operational data is crucial for building trust and compliance with data protection regulations such as GDPR (General Data Protection Regulation). Implementing strict data governance policies ensures that sensitive information is handled securely and transparently.

Corporate Governance and Accountability: Effective governance structures in warehousing also require leadership accountability, ethical decision-making, and adherence to laws and regulations. Having clear corporate governance structures that outline roles, responsibilities, and decision-making processes helps ensure that warehouses are operating in a manner that aligns with their ESG commitments.

2. Strategies for Integrating ESG Goals in Warehousing

Integrating ESG goals into warehousing operations requires a deliberate strategy and action plan. The following are key steps warehouses can take to align with ESG frameworks:

a. Setting Clear ESG Objectives

Before embarking on the integration of ESG goals, it is essential to establish clear, measurable objectives that align with the company's overall sustainability strategy. This might include setting goals for reducing carbon emissions, increasing the percentage of waste recycled, improving employee satisfaction, or enhancing supply chain transparency. Having specific, achievable goals allows companies to measure their progress and hold themselves accountable to stakeholders.

b. Sustainable Design and Green Certifications

One of the most effective ways to integrate ESG principles into warehousing is through the design and construction of sustainable facilities. This includes choosing energy-efficient construction materials, optimizing warehouse layouts for energy efficiency, and seeking certifications such as LEED, ISO 14001 (Environmental Management), or BREEAM. These certifications provide a framework for sustainable practices and demonstrate the company's commitment to environmental stewardship.

c. Supply Chain Collaboration and Partner Engagement

Warehouses can integrate ESG principles by working closely with suppliers, contractors, and logistics partners who share similar sustainability goals. Collaboration with partners allows for shared best practices, joint sustainability initiatives, and greater transparency across the supply chain. For example, a warehouse might collaborate with a shipping partner to reduce fuel consumption through optimized routing or engage with a supplier to use more sustainable packaging materials.

d. Employee Training and Engagement

To foster a culture of sustainability, warehouses must engage their employees in ESG efforts. This can be achieved through training programs focused on environmental stewardship, ethical labor practices, and the importance of safety and well-being. Engaging employees in sustainability initiatives not only helps achieve ESG goals but also strengthens employee morale and loyalty.

e. Reporting and Communication

Transparency is a critical aspect of ESG integration. Regularly reporting on ESG performance through annual sustainability reports or third-party audits ensures accountability and allows stakeholders, including investors, customers, and regulatory bodies, to assess a company's progress. Clear communication about sustainability efforts and achievements can also enhance a company's brand reputation and attract like-minded customers and partners.

3. Benefits and Challenges of Integrating ESG Goals in Warehousing

Integrating ESG goals into warehousing operations offers numerous benefits, but it also presents challenges that must be addressed.

a. Benefits

Cost Savings: Sustainable practices such as energy-efficient technologies, waste reduction, and efficient material handling can lead to significant cost savings over time. Reducing energy consumption and water usage, for example, can lower operating expenses.

Improved Reputation and Brand Loyalty: Customers and stakeholders are increasingly seeking companies that demonstrate a commitment to sustainability. By aligning with

ESG goals, warehouses can enhance their reputation, attract eco-conscious customers, and retain loyal employees.

Compliance and Risk Management: As regulations around environmental and social issues become stricter, warehouses that proactively integrate ESG goals can avoid potential fines, penalties, and reputational risks. Meeting or exceeding regulatory standards also positions the company as an industry leader.

b. Challenges

Initial Investment: Implementing sustainable technologies, training employees, and obtaining certifications often require significant upfront investments. For some warehouses, particularly small- to medium-sized operations, this can be a financial challenge.

Complexity of Integration: Integrating ESG goals across all areas of warehousing operations—from environmental practices to social policies—requires a comprehensive approach that may involve changes to business processes, supply chain management, and employee engagement strategies. Coordinating these changes can be complex and require careful planning.

Measuring Impact: Measuring the effectiveness of ESG initiatives can be challenging, especially in terms of quantifying social impacts or the long-term environmental benefits of certain practices. Developing clear metrics for ESG goals is crucial for tracking progress and demonstrating accountability.

Integrating ESG goals into warehousing operations is no longer optional but a necessary step toward long-term sustainability. By focusing on environmental responsibility, social impact, and strong governance, warehouses can contribute positively to society, reduce their environmental footprint, and enhance their business success. While the journey to full ESG integration may present challenges, the benefits far outweigh the costs, positioning companies for continued growth in an increasingly conscious global market.

Measuring and Reporting Sustainability Performance

In today's business landscape, companies are under increasing pressure to demonstrate their commitment to sustainability through measurable performance. This pressure comes not only from regulatory authorities but also from consumers, investors, and other stakeholders who are seeking transparency and accountability in corporate sustainability practices. Measuring and reporting sustainability performance involves the establishment of key performance indicators (KPIs), the use of audit tools, and the communication of results in a way that resonates with stakeholders. This chapter will focus on the importance of sustainability measurement, the most common KPIs used for assessing sustainability performance, and the tools and methods for conducting sustainability audits and reporting.

1. Importance of Measuring Sustainability Performance

Measuring sustainability performance is critical for several reasons:

Accountability: As companies face increasing scrutiny from both regulatory bodies and consumers, measuring sustainability ensures that a company can demonstrate its environmental, social, and governance (ESG) practices. It helps track progress and holds businesses accountable for their promises.

Improved Decision-Making: By measuring sustainability, companies gain insights into which areas are performing well and where improvement is needed. This data-driven approach allows businesses to make informed decisions on how to allocate resources, streamline operations, and invest in sustainability initiatives.

Competitive Advantage: Companies that can demonstrate strong sustainability performance differentiate themselves in the market. Investors are increasingly drawn to businesses with clear sustainability metrics, and consumers often prefer to support companies that align with their values on sustainability.

Risk Management: By regularly measuring sustainability performance, companies can identify potential risks related to environmental compliance, social issues, or governance failures before they become significant liabilities.

Legal and Regulatory Compliance: Many jurisdictions require companies to report on their sustainability performance. Adopting a clear framework for measuring sustainability ensures that a company remains in compliance with local and international regulations.

2. Key Performance Indicators (KPIs) for Sustainability

KPIs are quantifiable metrics that organizations use to assess their performance in achieving sustainability goals. They provide a clear picture of whether sustainability objectives are being met and help identify areas for improvement. The KPIs used to measure sustainability performance generally align with the three pillars of ESG: environmental impact, social responsibility, and governance practices.

a. Environmental KPIs

Environmental KPIs are designed to measure the ecological impact of a company's operations. These include metrics related to resource consumption, waste generation, carbon emissions, and energy efficiency.

Carbon Footprint (CO_2 Emissions): The total amount of greenhouse gases (GHGs) emitted directly or indirectly by a company, often measured in metric tons of CO_2 equivalent. This is one of the most critical environmental KPIs, as reducing carbon emissions is central to sustainability efforts.

Energy Consumption: The total amount of energy consumed in warehouse operations, typically measured in kilowatt-hours (kWh) or gigajoules (GJ). Companies track energy consumption to understand their energy efficiency and identify opportunities for reducing energy use.

Water Usage: The volume of water used by the company, often measured in cubic meters. Efficient water management practices, such as rainwater harvesting or using low-flow fixtures, can significantly reduce a company's water footprint.

Waste Diversion Rate: The percentage of waste that is diverted from landfills through recycling or other sustainable waste management practices. A higher diversion rate indicates better waste management and sustainability practices.

Material Recycled: The amount of materials, such as packaging or raw materials, that are recycled within a warehouse. This can include everything from recyclable packaging to scrap metal or paper products.

b. Social KPIs

Social KPIs measure a company's impact on its employees, customers, and the wider community. They focus on factors such as employee safety, well-being, diversity, and engagement, as well as the company's community involvement.

Employee Safety and Incident Rate: This includes the number of workplace accidents or injuries per a certain number of work hours (e.g., per 100,000 hours). A lower incident rate indicates a safer work environment and better employee welfare practices.

Employee Engagement and Satisfaction: Measured through surveys or turnover rates, employee engagement and satisfaction KPIs reflect how motivated, committed, and productive employees are within the company. High engagement levels often correlate with improved organizational performance and a positive workplace culture.

Diversity and Inclusion: Metrics related to workforce diversity, including gender, race, and ethnicity breakdowns, can help track progress toward inclusivity in the workplace. KPIs could include the percentage of minority groups in leadership positions or gender pay equity.

Community Investment: The amount of money or resources a company invests in local communities through charity, outreach programs, or educational initiatives. This can include volunteer hours, donations, or direct investments in social causes.

c. Governance KPIs

Governance KPIs focus on a company's governance structure, including leadership, transparency, and ethical conduct. These KPIs ensure that a company is operating in a responsible and ethical manner.

Board Diversity: This measures the diversity of the company's board of directors in terms of gender, race, and other demographics. A diverse board ensures varied perspectives and enhances the governance process.

Compliance and Ethics Violations: The number of ethical breaches or regulatory violations within a company. Lower rates of violations indicate strong governance practices and adherence to laws and regulations.

Transparency and Reporting: This KPI evaluates the company's commitment to transparency in its ESG performance. Companies can measure this by the frequency and detail of their sustainability reporting, including third-party audits or certifications.

3. Tools for Sustainability Audits and Reporting

To ensure accurate measurement and reporting, companies often rely on various tools and frameworks for sustainability audits. These tools help companies track progress toward their sustainability goals, assess compliance, and communicate results effectively to stakeholders.

a. Sustainability Audits

A sustainability audit is a comprehensive evaluation of a company's practices and processes to assess how well it is meeting its sustainability objectives. The audit looks at environmental, social, and governance practices across the entire organization. Audits are typically performed by external auditors or sustainability consultants who provide an objective, unbiased evaluation of performance.

Environmental Impact Audits: These audits assess the company's environmental performance by reviewing practices related to energy use, waste management, emissions, and resource consumption. They help identify areas where improvements can be made and provide recommendations for reducing the environmental impact.

Social and Labor Audits: These audits focus on assessing the company's labor practices, including employee safety, fair wages, working conditions, and diversity and inclusion policies.

They are often conducted by third-party organizations that specialize in human rights and social accountability.

Supply Chain Audits: Conducted to ensure that suppliers and contractors align with the company's sustainability goals, supply chain audits assess the environmental and social practices of key suppliers and subcontractors.

b. Reporting Frameworks and Standards

Once sustainability performance has been measured, companies need to communicate their findings clearly and consistently to stakeholders. Several reporting frameworks and standards are widely used in the industry for sustainability reporting.

Global Reporting Initiative (GRI): GRI provides a comprehensive set of guidelines for sustainability reporting. It helps companies disclose environmental, social, and governance impacts in a standardized and transparent manner.

Sustainability Accounting Standards Board (SASB): SASB focuses on industry-specific sustainability disclosures that are financially material to investors. It provides a framework for companies to disclose relevant ESG factors that may affect financial performance.

Carbon Disclosure Project (CDP): The CDP is an international non-profit organization that encourages companies to disclose their environmental impact. It provides a standardized format for companies to report their greenhouse gas emissions, water usage, and climate-related risks.

Integrated Reporting (IR): IR combines financial and non-financial information into a cohesive report, providing a comprehensive picture of the company's value creation over time. It integrates ESG considerations with traditional financial performance metrics.

ISO 14001 (Environmental Management): ISO 14001 provides a framework for creating and maintaining an effective environmental management system (EMS). It helps organizations measure and manage their environmental impact and ensures compliance with environmental regulations.

4. Challenges in Measuring and Reporting Sustainability Performance

While measuring and reporting sustainability performance is essential for transparency and accountability, companies may face several challenges in this process.

Data Availability and Quality: Reliable data is critical for accurate sustainability measurement. However, many companies struggle with obtaining consistent, high-quality data, particularly in areas like supply chain impacts and social metrics. Ensuring data accuracy and consistency can be a significant challenge.

Complexity of Reporting: Sustainability reporting often involves complex calculations, especially in areas like carbon emissions and waste reduction. Many companies lack the internal expertise or systems to track and report sustainability data comprehensively.

Regulatory and Reporting Differences: Different jurisdictions have varying requirements for sustainability reporting, which can make it difficult for global companies to comply with multiple regulations. This lack of standardization can lead to confusion or non-compliance.

Stakeholder Expectations: As stakeholder expectations around sustainability continue to rise, companies may feel pressure to report on a wide range of ESG issues. Balancing transparency with the ability to present meaningful, actionable information can be challenging.

Measuring and reporting sustainability performance is an essential aspect of any company's sustainability strategy. By setting clear KPIs, utilizing sustainability audit tools, and following established reporting frameworks, companies can ensure they are making tangible progress toward their sustainability goals. Moreover, transparent and consistent reporting helps build trust with stakeholders, improves decision-making, and enhances the company's competitive position in the market. As businesses continue to prioritize sustainability, effective measurement and reporting will become even more critical for ensuring long-term success and accountability.

Conclusion: The Path Forward

Sustainable warehousing is no longer a niche or optional consideration for businesses; it has become a vital aspect of modern operations. As the global focus on sustainability intensifies, the role of warehouses in driving environmental, social, and economic performance has gained unprecedented importance. This chapter has explored the essential elements of sustainable warehousing, from energy-efficient building designs to the integration of renewable energy, efficient material handling, and the use of innovative technologies like IoT and automation. We have also highlighted the importance of workforce engagement, the adoption of circular economy principles, and the measurement and reporting of sustainability performance.

Recap of Key Concepts

Green Building Design: Sustainable warehouse design emphasizes energy efficiency, natural lighting, renewable energy sources, and the use of eco-friendly materials. These principles help reduce the carbon footprint of warehouse operations and contribute to a more sustainable built environment.

Energy Management: The integration of renewable energy solutions like solar panels, wind turbines, and geothermal energy plays a crucial role in reducing reliance on non-renewable sources. Energy-efficient technologies, along with energy monitoring systems, enable warehouses to reduce electricity consumption and improve overall operational efficiency.

Water Conservation: Water-saving strategies, including rainwater harvesting and low-flow fixtures, reduce a warehouse's environmental impact by conserving one of the planet's most precious resources.

Waste Management: Sustainable waste management practices, such as reducing, reusing, and recycling waste, are key to creating efficient, eco-friendly warehouse operations. Proper management of packaging materials also reduces waste generation and encourages circularity in warehouse processes.

Technological Innovation: The use of automation, IoT, big data, and advanced warehouse management systems (WMS) further enhances sustainability efforts by optimizing resource utilization, improving energy efficiency, and reducing waste.

Transportation and Logistics: Eco-friendly transportation strategies, including the adoption of electric and hybrid vehicles, as well as optimized route planning, are essential for reducing the carbon footprint of logistics operations.

Workforce Engagement: Building a culture of sustainability through training, collaboration, and community engagement fosters long-term commitment to green practices within warehouse operations. Additionally, embracing ESG (Environmental, Social, and Governance) goals ensures that warehousing aligns with broader corporate responsibility strategies.

Call to Action for Sustainable Warehousing Practices

The transition to sustainable warehousing is not only a strategic move for companies looking to reduce costs and enhance their brand value; it is a responsibility towards the environment and future generations. The practices and principles outlined throughout this book provide a robust framework for warehouses aiming to improve their sustainability performance. However, simply adopting sustainable measures is not enough. A continuous commitment to improvement, innovation, and adaptation is necessary to ensure long-term success.

1. Invest in Green Technologies: Companies must prioritize investment in energy-efficient technologies, renewable energy solutions, and automation systems that enhance both operational efficiency and sustainability.

2. Set Clear Sustainability Goals and KPIs: Establishing measurable sustainability targets and monitoring progress is crucial. This includes setting specific goals for energy consumption, waste reduction, water usage, and carbon emissions, with a clear roadmap for achieving them.

3. Foster a Culture of Sustainability: Engaging employees at all levels, from management to operational staff, ensures that sustainability becomes ingrained in the company's culture. Continuous training and awareness campaigns can help embed green practices into everyday operations.

4. Collaborate with Stakeholders: Building partnerships with local communities, suppliers, and customers is essential for fostering shared responsibility in achieving sustainability goals. Transparent reporting and open communication will help build trust with stakeholders.

5. Measure, Report, and Improve: Regular sustainability audits and transparent reporting ensure that businesses can track their progress, make data-driven decisions, and demonstrate accountability. Regular reviews of performance will help identify areas for further improvement.

6. Prepare for the Future: Sustainability is an ongoing journey. Emerging trends, technologies, and consumer expectations will continue to evolve. Companies must remain adaptable, constantly looking for new opportunities to enhance their sustainability practices.

In conclusion, sustainable warehousing represents a path forward for companies that wish to stay ahead of the curve in an increasingly eco-conscious world. By implementing the strategies discussed and making sustainability a core part of operations, warehouses can play a pivotal role in driving the green economy while delivering financial, operational, and reputational benefits. Now is the time for businesses to act and set the standard for sustainable warehousing practices in the 21st century. The future of warehousing is green—let's take the necessary steps to shape it today.

"Sustainability in warehousing isn't just about reducing footprints—it's about leaving lasting imprints of responsibility, innovation, and progress for generations to come."

www.ingramcontent.com/pod-product-compliance
Lightning Source LLC
Chambersburg PA
CBHW071020240526
45469CB00006BD/2015